JAN 1 1 2006

# DIVORCE
# WAR!

D1364952

# DIVORCE WAR!

## 50 STRATEGIES EVERY WOMAN NEEDS TO KNOW TO WIN

Bradley A. Pistotnik, Esq.

ADAMS MEDIA CORPORATION
Avon, Massachusetts

Published by Adams Media, an F+W Publications Company
57 Littlefield Street, Avon, MA 02322. U.S.A.
*www. adamsmedia.com*

ISBN: 1-55850-600-4

Printed in the United States of America.

J  I  H  G  F

Library of Congress Cataloging-in-Publication Data
Pistotnik, Bradley A.
Divorce war! : 50 strategies every woman needs to know to win /
by Bradley A. Pistotnik.
p.    cm.
Includes index.
ISBN 1-55850-600-4 (pbk.)
1. Divorce suits—United States—Popular works. I. Title.
KF535.Z9P57    1996
346.7301'66—dc20
[347.306166]            96–2366
CIP

This publication is designed to provide accurate and authoritative information with regard to the subject matter covered. It is sold with the understanding that the publisher is not engaged in rendering legal, accounting, or other professional advice. If legal advice or other expert assistance is required, the services of a competent professional person should be sought.
— From a *Declaration of Principles* jointly adopted by a Committee of the American Bar Association and a Committee of Publishers and Associations

*This book is available at quantity discounts for bulk purchases.*
*For information, call 1-800-872-5627.*

# *Dedication*

I dedicate this book to my loving wife, Candice, who supported me every step of the way in writing this book. It is she who convinced me that this book could help women in all walks of life regardless of their situation. Without her love, patience, and comment, this book would not exist. I further dedicate this book to my mother, JoAnn. But for her guidance, teaching, and loving, I would not have been able to write and create. Finally, I dedicate this book to our heavenly Father above, who allows each and every one of us a second chance at life.

# Table of Contents

# Table of Contents

## Part Two

## Are You Ready for Battle?

# Table of Contents

# *Introduction*

This book was written to enable women to develop strategies for getting what they want and deserve in their divorces. Generally, women trust the advice of their counsel in determining what is fair in a divorce settlement. However, this is not a good idea—not all lawyers are created equal. If a woman has an incompetent divorce lawyer, she can lose everything—her home, her children, her marital assets, and everything else she once possessed.

The strategies, rules, advice, and belief systems expressed in this book are not advocated by all lawyers. Ethics plays a substantial role in any legal advice. Information in this book is not necessarily meant to be advice to you as the reader, but is intended to inform you of the choices that can be made in your divorce to help you obtain a fair settlement.

Law is not always just. A lawyer's understanding of the legal statutes and case laws concerning domestic issues does not mean that his client will obtain a fair award. With this in mind, a woman seeking a divorce must be involved—not only to develop and implement a strategy, but to gather information to prove her case.

After years of practice, I have developed strategies that will help you to succeed in your divorce. They have nothing to do with legal statutes or case law. Instead, they are informational, psychological, and strategic steps that you can utilize to convince a judge that you deserve a larger share of the divorce pie. By controlling the methods you use, you can influence the outcome of your divorce.

In recent years, marital law has changed. With the emergence of marital torts, women who have been unloved, abused, and neglected now have greater legal recourse during a divorce proceeding. A tort is a wrongful, injurious, or damaging act not involving a breach of contract for which a civil action can be brought. In the last two decades, a number of states have allowed wives to sue their husbands for marital torts. In years past, one spouse could not sue the other even if an injury was caused. However, this concept, which was known as marital immunity, has now been abolished.

A marital tort suit allows a wife to tip the scales of justice in her favor. For example, a prenuptial contract that limits the wife's recovery after a divorce may prevent the divorce settlement from being fair, but a marital tort suit can rectify the inequity of a marriage contract. Not all divorces present good cases for a marital tort, but any marriage that has been volatile or harmful will most likely present a basis to file a marital tort. Fortunately, the days in which the courts overlooked spousal abuse are now over. If you have been harmed, emotionally or physically, you now have legal recourse.

Because little has been written on this topic, many divorce lawyers fail to utilize the legal theories that these new developments have generated. Lawyers tend to opt for the easiest route, and taking on an additional marital tort suit may not be on your lawyer's agenda. However, you need to find out all you can about this additional weapon in your divorce armory, so that you—not your lawyer—can be the one to make a rational decision about whether to accept a given divorce settlement or file a marital tort case.

I've provided case histories throughout the book to illustrate the importance of these strategies. After reading this book,

# Introduction

you will understand how to create a plan in your best interests. You will have the knowledge you need to protect yourself so that you can get more from your husband and the legal system.

I've written this book because my experience shows that people need more information about divorce. If you have been married only once, you will have had no experience to enable you to understand what happens in a divorce. After representing women (and men) in hundreds of divorces, I realize how helpless a woman can feel during divorce proceedings. Obtaining a divorce is one of life's most tragic events, often as emotionally painful as the death of a loved one. It is particularly sad to think that after all the pain you have experienced, you might come away from your marriage with less than you deserve because your lawyer chose the path of least resistance.

If you have bought this book, you have enough knowledge, self-esteem, and intellect to want to learn how to protect yourself and your assets. The advice in the following chapters will furnish you with the necessary tools to empower you and help you win your divorce.

Not all lawyers necessarily advocate the strategies, rules, and advice expressed in this book. Some of them may seem aggressive, and even deceitful. Nevertheless, keep in mind that they may be your only way to rectify the injustices that have been committed against you. Factual portrayals in the case histories establish basic patterns of conduct that divorced couples have gone through while fighting for individual rights. Just because an instance has been portrayed does not mean that I advocate the positions taken by the parties.

While I believe that all of the practices outlined in this book are a part of today's divorce world, I expressly caution all readers not to rely on this book as exact legal advice. You should seek local legal advice from your own counsel.

Many of the practices described in this book may have ethical ramifications. For that reason, I caution you, the reader, that the information contained in this book cannot always be used in all circumstances. The information is not intended to be direct legal advice to you. The fact that individuals have acted out the practices described in the book does not mean that they are legally advised to you as a client. You must establish a lawyer–client relationship with a lawyer in your area who is familiar with your local laws.

Finally, this book merely brings to light some suggestions and depicts some of the particularly interesting or traumatic divorce situations that I have encountered. The information in this book was accurate upon publication, but laws change, and you should consult with your state bar or your attorney.

**Part One** | *What You Should Know Before You File*

# Chapter 1 | *A Crucial Decision: To Play Fair or Tough?*

## Do You Really Want a Divorce?

Ultimately, only you can know whether you want a divorce. Ask yourself these critical questions: Has your husband committed adultery? Has he abused you physically or emotionally? Do you feel his commitment to his work takes priority over you? Does he give you the attention and love you need and want? Does he stay out late with his friends and treat you without the respect you deserve? Or do you find that after years of marriage the love between you has faded and now you want the freedom to find a new man who *will* fulfill your needs? Are you simply bored and ready to move on?

You have been at your husband's side for years, supporting him emotionally and helping him reach his financial and career goals. Now that you are considering a divorce, you realize that he has all the assets and the ability to go on making a good living, even though you were an integral part of his success. Will you be able to reap any benefit from the years of support you have provided? Will you be able to receive your hard-earned fair share? Keep in mind that justice is not always fair. You *could* walk away from a marriage with little or nothing to start your life over.

Once you have decided that the time is ripe to plan for divorce, you can significantly improve your chances of getting what you deserve. But to accomplish this, you need strategy, planning, and help.

## Should You Profit at Your Husband's Expense?

Traditionally, women were not involved in the management of their family's finances. They learned to let men make the decisions, especially in money matters. Women today have become increasingly responsible for their family's finances. In many situations, women work not just because they want to, but because they have to. Yet often they remain unaware of their own family's overall financial picture.

Whether you work or not, it is absolutely crucial that you ask your husband about insurance, wills, bank accounts, and other pertinent financial information.

Always remember that you have a right and an obligation to be involved in the finances of your marriage and family. Do not let your husband brush you off when you ask him financially related questions. It is important that you take the initiative and learn about this aspect of your life.

Many women say, "Oh, my husband would never cheat me or treat me badly or keep me from getting what I deserve." But think of all the stories you hear where exactly this happens. You must protect yourself because no one else will.

Your lawyer certainly won't. He is primarily concerned with getting his fee. Your husband will definitely not be concerned with protecting you after you ask for a divorce. His only mission will be to safeguard his assets and protect himself. Only you have the ability to plan an effective strategy and win the divorce war. Forget what you have been taught in the past. Now is the time to educate yourself and hone your skills for battle.

## A Crucial Decision: To Play Fair or Tough?

In order to protect yourself and your children, you should remember that most men exist in the world of business, where logic and numbers ultimately define the winners and losers. Their daily practice of winning in the competitive business world gives them a natural edge when fighting a divorce. With this in mind, you must attempt to level the playing field by learning businesslike tactics. You certainly don't want to be underskilled when the divorce process begins.

You don't necessarily have to profit at your husband's expense. But after years of loyalty to him, you do have a right to receive an equal share of the total marital assets. Obtaining a divorce award is not a mischievous ambition. Potentially, the award you receive will provide you with the largest amount of property distribution and the longest term of alimony, both of which will help you in your new life. Your husband is going to survive the divorce. Will you? Remind yourself that there is nothing wrong with structuring your divorce so that in the long run, both of you survive and get back on your feet.

Was your husband a good-for-nothing rake during the marriage? If so, maybe you *should* profit from the divorce. Is he planning to marry the longtime girlfriend you only recently found out about? Then why give him more income to support, clothe, and house her in your home? The less disposable income he has to spend on her, the more satisfied you can be. For each dollar he loses, you should be able to gain a dollar. You should go for at least half of everything. Ultimately, there is little difference between obtaining a profit and receiving your fair share.

A divorce judge, however, just might decide that you deserve little alimony to start over. In fact, if you are employable and have no extreme mental duress from the marriage, most courts will see little reason to award you long-term alimony. The current nationwide trend is toward short-term alimony just to get a woman back on her feet. Typically, this is called rehabilitative maintenance or alimony.

Many factors affect the court's decision on what property should be given to a wife. Some factors allow the court to rule that you do not get much of your husband's property. If you let the court award you less than a fair share, your husband has beaten you in the biggest battle of your divorce war.

Your role as a housewife or a working wife may play a substantial part in how much you are able to ultimately receive. This is because a court attempts to be equitable to both sides in a divorce. Income produced by you will provide the judge a basis for ordering less alimony or child support. When you are working there is no real need for rehabilitative maintenance to help you get back on your feet.

Of course, the disparity between your income and your husband's will be taken into consideration. The wider the gap, the greater your chance of obtaining a larger settlement.

Does this mean that a wife working at home as a housewife will receive more in a divorce settlement than a wife working outside the home? Each case is unique to its own specific facts. Because of the case-by-case analysis utilized by courts, this one factor may not be a sole deciding issue for the judge. However, as a general rule, a working wife may receive less than a housewife in a similar situation.

## Revenge Is Sweet

No matter how nice your husband has been, once he has caused you to seek a divorce, it is time to fight. It doesn't matter if he never abused you or cheated on you. Maybe he treated you like a queen. But when he stopped providing his love to you—for whatever reason—you lost almost everything (except your children) in the marriage. Loss of love is a catastrophe. Revenge is all that is left to you.

Perhaps this philosophy seems a bit cynical. Well, you may be the sweetest woman in the world—but are you going to let him take your soul, pull it out, and stomp on it until your feelings are dead? Don't do that to yourself. There is no reason for you to feel guilty about protecting yourself.

Husbands are well aware that if they play, they are going to pay. Husbands almost readily accept the fact that they will be punished if caught. Money is the bargaining chip that wives use to punish their husbands. Remember, you can be spending his hard-earned cash with your new lover, rather than watching him spend his savings on his new wife.

## Create a Master Battle Plan

By following the strategy proposed in this book, you will learn to prepare a master battle plan for your divorce. Without this knowledge, you will be at the mercy of your lawyer and the judicial system.

What if you don't find the right lawyer? Locating a good lawyer is difficult. Alas, some are lazy, don't keep up with the law, and are more concerned with themselves than with their cases. Do not forget: If your lawyer handles your case without your supervision and input, he will have total control over your future. If you don't stay apprised of your case, you might as well go out and spend money on lottery tickets.

When you know the rules of the game and what your lawyer is supposed to be doing, you will be able to control your own destiny. Never put your life in the hands of another person. If you do, it will be the single biggest mistake you will ever make. You only get one chance to win. When the divorce award is made by the judge, it is too late to change it. You can appeal, but the first decision made by a judge is rarely overturned.

Learning how to prepare the evidence to convince the judge that you should win is the most difficult component of the plan. The more you know about your husband's activities and assets, his weaknesses, and his own plan, the better off you will be.

Preparation for your divorce is the most important test of your life. Studying for a college exam is easy—the information is readily available from textbooks and study aids. Studying for your divorce test is far more difficult. All of the information needed to ace the test is hidden. You have to dig for it. No one has ever taught you how to prepare for divorce. Evidence to prove you should win must be established in your favor—or you lose.

## Fifty Strategies of Divorce

All of the strategies which will be discussed in the following chapters are set out below. Each strategy will be thoroughly discussed with examples and case histories to illustrate its importance.

**Strategy 1.** Planning for your divorce requires a minimum of six months.

**Strategy 2.** Never trust that your husband has provided you with full or accurate information about his assets and financial situation.

**Strategy 3.** Hire the toughest, best-liked, and most highly connected lawyer money can buy.

**Strategy 4.** Save at least five thousand dollars. You may need it for your attorney.

**Strategy 5.** Challenge your prenuptial or postnuptial contract whenever you have any real basis for challenge, regardless how small.

**Strategy 6.** Never confide your plan to a relative or friend, no matter how close you are to them.

**Strategy 7.** Find and review your husband's tax returns.

**Strategy 8.** To win in court, you must have evidence. Copy every bit of financial evidence about your husband's assets that you can locate.

**Strategy 9.** Checks and deposit slips tell a story about your husband that you never knew.

**Strategy 10.** Be clever and shrewd. Ask the right questions and be friendly with all of your husband's financial advisors, stockbrokers, attorneys, and secretaries.

**Strategy 11.** The first person to make it to the courthouse has the better chance of winning the divorce war.

**Strategy 12.** You must build a financial cushion prior to filing for divorce so you will not suffer during and following your divorce.

**Strategy 13.** Always determine valid reasons why you had to withdraw cash from a joint or individual account to prevent the court from ordering you to give the money back.

**Strategy 14.** Never perpetrate a fraud upon the court, or your best-laid plans will backfire.

**Strategy 15.** Use accurate financial records during divorce proceedings so the court will award the proper temporary and permanent alimony.

**Strategy 16.** Never make a blackmail attempt upon your husband. A judge can hold this against you in the final award of property.

**Strategy 17.** The more you and your husband save, the more you get in the divorce trial.

**Strategy 18.** Be unemployed for as long a period of time as possible prior to filing for divorce.

**Strategy 19.** The longer you are unemployed before filing for divorce, the better your chances are of receiving long-term alimony.

**Strategy 20.** The level of child support payments will be determined by three factors: how many children you have, how high your husband's income is, and how low your own income is.

Strategy 21.  Be certain to hire a psychologist who is well recognized by your local divorce judges.

Strategy 22.  When you want a divorce, learn to aggravate your husband whenever possible, but never engage in conduct that might be construed as detrimental to your position in the divorce.

Strategy 23.  Get all credit cards in your husband's name to limit your liability for the debt after the divorce. You should be careful to understand that cash advances should be used to aid the marital estate and not to rob the estate of assets. You are never advised to perjure yourself before the court by stating an alternative purpose other than what is true.

Strategy 24.  Control your husband by being alternately loving and indifferent to keep him in a state of continual concern.

Strategy 25.  Every divorce case has a silver lining. The mental stress caused by your husband provides a basis to sue for a marital tort.

Strategy 26.  A marital tort suit may allow you to receive more than your marriage contract agrees to.

Strategy 27.  Use fault against your husband as an additional means to win your divorce.

Strategy 28.  Before claiming your husband's alcohol or drug abuse, examine your own usage.

Strategy 29.  Photographic and videotaped evidence is far better than a live witness.

Strategy 30.  Never tape-record your husband over the telephone without first consulting your divorce lawyer.

Strategy 31.  Hire a detective who specializes in matrimonial investigation.

**Strategy 32.** Hire a detective to prove your husband has a bad character, and pay for the services with your husband's money.

**Strategy 33.** When you hire a detective, do not pay him by check. Keep his knowledge and existence confidential.

**Strategy 34.** Never verbalize anything that you do not want repeated in court.

**Strategy 35.** Never trust anyone else. This includes your mother, sister, best friend, and divorce lawyer. Shocking as it may seem, anyone of them could betray you.

**Strategy 36.** Never write down your plan or keep any written documentation that might establish a plan's existence.

**Strategy 37.** Without question, hire the sharpest, most intelligent, skilled trial attorney who also handles matrimonial law.

**Strategy 38.** Always ask for more than what is fair, and substantially more than you think you deserve.

**Strategy 39.** Always hire an expert who will stand by your side of the case.

**Strategy 40.** Hire the best psychologist you can find.

**Strategy 41.** Always maintain a business relationship with your psychologist and other experts.

**Strategy 42.** In court, dress conservatively and act in a conservative manner.

**Strategy 43.** Be certain to consult with your lawyer about the effect of your husband's filing for bankruptcy after your divorce as it relates to your division of the marital estate.

**Strategy 44.** Assume long-term debt obligations—if the court awards alimony to cover the debt, and if you are allowed to retain the property.

**Strategy 45.** Always keep a log of cash payments made to you by your husband, including the reasons the payments were made.

**Strategy 46.** Structure your divorce settlement to minimize tax liability.

**Strategy 47.** When seeking alimony in a property settlement agreement, contractually agree with your husband to minimize the contingent events that may terminate your right to alimony.

**Strategy 48.** To protect your alimony, child custody, and child support, avoid cohabiting with a member of the opposite sex.

**Strategy 49.** When preparing your plan for divorce, be certain that you have properly determined all goals you desire to reach.

**Strategy 50.** You need to go all out to win your divorce the first time, because appeals are rarely won.

# Chapter 2 | *Plan Your Escape*

Like most women, you will not decide to leave your marriage without undergoing a long period of painful and agonizing consideration. But when at last you make this very difficult determination, it is time to start planning your escape.

---

**Strategy 1.** *Planning for your divorce requires a minimum of six months.*

---

Once you have made up your mind to divorce, you must stay married long enough to develop your master plan. It may take months, even years, to formulate the appropriate methods and procedures. But just as a general in charge of an army does not simply move in and attack, you cannot plunge into a divorce battle without planning ahead. You must also develop a tactical strategy in order to win the war.

Always remember that every minute of planning you spend on your divorce will ultimately help you gain more compensation. Carefully consider how much time is required. The time you spend planning your divorce will depend on how much your husband is worth. The more assets he has, the more time you will need to develop your plan.

Planning for your divorce is much like cooking spaghetti sauce from scratch. Sure, you can buy the sauce in a jar. It won't taste as good, but it will suffice. Do you want your divorce to simply suffice, or do you want it to reflect your meticulous planning and hard work? In other words, do you want to win the divorce, receive long-term alimony, and obtain a hefty property settlement?

***Strategy 2.*** *Never trust that your husband has provided you with full or accurate information about his assets and financial situation.*

Regardless of how much your husband is worth, you need to carefully investigate his financial situation. Proving his hidden wealth is particularly difficult, because most likely he has made an effort to conceal his financial affairs. If you don't take the necessary time to research this aspect of your case, your husband will end up winning.

## Wealthy Husbands Require Long-Term Planning

Those of you who are married to a wealthy man will especially benefit from thorough planning. The rationale is simple. If you research and uncover more of your husband's assets, you can receive more of them in the divorce settlement.

Let's suppose that your husband has a stock portfolio, investment accounts, IRAs, Keogh plans, and other retirement or profit-sharing plans, in addition to homes, vehicles, and other personal property. You can, with proper planning, attempt to shift substantial portions of these monetary assets into your name prior to filing for divorce.

While putting an asset in your name will not be the single determining factor for the court, there are certain instances where it will definitely be a boon in the final outcome of your divorce. Vehicle titles, IRAs, and independent investments or stock portfolios may all be kept in your name.

You may not be aware of all the assets your husband owns. If he is a shrewd businessman, he may own stock in many different types of corporations to ensure a distribution of his earnings and assets. Earnings from these various stocks can be difficult to find. The techniques discussed in subsequent chapters will help you find the majority, if not all, of his assets.

Keep in mind that these assets belong to both of you, and although he may not agree with the concept of joint ownership, you may be awarded half or all of the assets. In a community property state you should be awarded half, while in an equitable distribution state you may be awarded anywhere from 100 percent ownership interest to as little as no ownership interest. These concepts are discussed later in the book.

The point to remember is simple. You can be awarded more assets if you know about more assets. When those assets are hidden from you, there is absolutely no way you have a chance of being awarded any part of them.

Starting today, you can begin to evaluate your husband's financial circumstances. For example, if he drives a five-year-old Cadillac with payments still due on it, the financial picture may be very different from one in which he drives a Mercedes 500 SL that has been paid for entirely. Many women mistakenly assume that their husbands are worth more or less than they actually are. Make sure that you make no assumptions and find out the hard facts so you can protect yourself.

## Middle-Class Husbands Need Shrewd Strategy

If, like the majority of American women, you are a member of the middle class, you must also plan effectively to protect yourself after a divorce. The strategies of this book apply equally to your marital situation. Some may simply have a greater financial impact if your husband is wealthier.

The manner of asset distribution is different for middle-class husbands. Typically, at this societal and financial level, most assets are tied up with debts such as car and house payments or other debt against property. With a middle-class husband, you must strive to obtain alimony, as well as equity from your home and your profit-sharing and retirement accounts.

Regardless of these differences, there are many ways to find divisible assets. If your husband is in middle or upper management in corporate America, he probably receives many fringe benefits. He may receive profit-sharing, retirement, stock-purchase, and other employment plans that you can claim as your own.

You should always attempt to gain as many of these assets as possible, because the courts will usually distribute them equitably between husband and wife. Although your husband may not yet have a vested interest in these assets, a court can make an order against his employer, granting you a portion when he starts to receive them. Remember, even if you have to wait, it is better to have a nest egg for your future than nothing at all.

## Blue-Collar Husbands Need the Least Planning

If you are married to a man with a blue-collar job, you will not need to plan as thoroughly as if you were married to a middle- or upper-class man. Nevertheless, the Strategies still apply to you even if the end result is not as lucrative. You can't draw blood from a turnip, but you should still get everything you deserve.

Your primary sources are child support, alimony, the division of equity from your home, and the retirement funds from your husband's employer, if any.

Perhaps you have been married to a military man who has been in the service long enough to receive retirement pay. Military husbands who divorce most often end up battling over these government accounts. Your job is to convince a court that you are entitled to half of his retirement funds. His military retirement account will be your long-term pot of gold. Remind yourself that in a divorce war, everything is fair.

The Strategy regarding employability, which will be discussed further in following chapters, will most likely not apply to you. In your case, in order to have financial stability you will need to be employed. As the adage goes, it takes so much dough to make a round cookie. You will be able to obtain a portion of that dough by following the advice in this book. The other portion will have to come from employment or another marriage.

Nevertheless, don't be discouraged. Every man, regardless of his social or financial status, shelters as much money as he possibly can, and if you learn every conceivable strategy and method, you can potentially obtain a significant portion of it.

## Chapter 3 | *Find the Best Divorce Lawyer*

Domestic law is at the same time the easiest and the most difficult law to practice. Law in this area does not change rapidly, and because of this slow evolution, the practice of law within it can be rather simplistic. Most lawyers who do not become specialized tend to lean toward the domestic field.

Yet successful matrimonial law depends on the development of shrewd and sometimes complicated strategies. Often lawyers who practice domestic law are unaware of this need for strategy and treat a divorce case like a game of darts. A lawyer may simply throw as many facts and theories at the judge as possible to see which one sticks. To win a divorce case, however, a lawyer needs to have a preformulated plan of attack.

---

*Strategy 3.*    *Hire the toughest, best-liked, and most highly connected lawyer money can buy.*

---

A major problem with something simple like domestic law is that a simpleton can learn it and claim expertise. Many of the lawyers practicing domestic law lack the skills shared by specialized trial lawyers who practice more complicated areas of law. Lawyers who advertise that they are experts in domestic law may not be experts at all. Don't take their assertions at face value. Dig deep. Question the lawyer about his or her specific skills, abilities, and number of cases represented and won. Once you have asked these questions, you will be able to make an educated and informed decision.

How articulate is the lawyer? Does he speak to you in incomprehensible legal terms? Remember, even a parrot can be trained to spew forth legal terms with no real understanding of their definitions. Many lawyers are like parrots in that they simply say these words without fully comprehending them in order to impress or purposely baffle others. Often, they feel that their lofty use of legal terminology makes them appear more capable than they really are. Keep in mind that arrogance and egotism befall the legal profession—don't allow this to influence your decision.

Furthermore, does the lawyer give any reasons why you should expect a certain decision by the court, and can he explain to you what that decision means? Can he recite statutes and case laws off the top of his head? Does he know in which direction a given judge may lean? You should consider all of these elements when making your determination.

## Talk to Other Women

Finding the right divorce lawyer who won't sell you down the river for thousands of dollars in legal fees is a difficult task. The best lawyers charge an arm and a leg—can you really afford to lose yours? The trick is to find a reasonably priced, qualified lawyer who won't charge more for his services than is warranted.

If you have friends who have divorced, they will be able to share their success ratio with you. Perhaps you belong to a civic or business organization, church, or other association where women gather. By speaking to divorced women in these groups, you will quickly learn that there are only a handful of recommended divorce lawyers in your city. Talk to no fewer than ten of these women and ask how favorable their divorce settlement was. If you find that a high percentage of these women have used the same lawyer and won their divorce cases, you know you are on the right track.

If several lawyers are recommended to you, make appointments with all of them and inquire about their experience and opinions on the potential outcome of your case. While the following questions will help you establish which lawyer has the necessary experience, you will still want to rely on your instincts to make your final choice.

1. How long has the lawyer practiced in the field of divorce law? As a general rule, you want a lawyer with no less than ten years of experience in the area of domestic practice combined with trial practice in other areas.

2. What other areas does the lawyer practice in? A jack-of-all-trades can be a big mistake. However, if the lawyer practices in a few select other areas involving trial work, this will make him a better divorce lawyer. The more he knows about civil procedural rules, the better a lawyer he will be. Surprisingly, many lawyers are not at all familiar with civil rules of procedure. Beware the lawyer who does not know the rules of practice!

3. Does the lawyer have a strong relationship with the divorce judges in your city? Does he or she have a relationship on a first-name basis with the judge? Do they play golf, tennis, or otherwise socialize together? The stronger the relationship, the better off you are with the lawyer. It's not always what you know, but who you know. In legal societies, the "good old boy" system still exists pretty much as it did a century ago.

4. How many clients does the lawyer routinely represent at one time? If a lawyer takes on too many clients, he

or she will not have time for your case. If a lawyer has more than 100 to 150 active cases, he may be in over his head. There is a high likelihood that your case will be shifted to an associate lawyer within the firm.

5.  Does the lawyer promise to work on your file and not assign it to an underling? If you cannot obtain this agreement, do not hire the lawyer. Bigger domestic lawyers act as rainmakers. A rainmaker is a lawyer who brings clients into the firm and then passes them off to other lawyers. Remember that lawyers are like cars. They come in all sizes, shapes, molds, and levels of ability. If you hired a Rolls-Royce lawyer, don't settle for a battered pickup truck. Stay with the lawyer who was recommended to you, and make sure that he states in writing that your case will only be handled by him.

6.  Does the lawyer place enough credence in your case that he requires no retainer of fees, or only a nominal retainer with the goal of obtaining the fees from your husband? If the lawyer won't do either of these things, he may not believe in your case.

7.  Does the lawyer put his contract in writing, or does he simply make an oral agreement? You want any contract with the lawyer to be in writing.

8.  What percentage of clients are male or female? It's okay if the lawyer represents substantially more women. But if he represents more men, his own personal philosophies may come into play, leaving you with a lawyer who is more sympathetic to the opposition. A female lawyer might have stronger allegiance to your side, although this is not always the case. A lawyer with a percentage of both male and female clients, but with a consistent empathy toward women's situations, will be best for you.

9. Can the lawyer accurately tell you the number of cases he has won? If tells you he always wins, you can assume he is lying. No one always wins. Ask him to give you the names of his cases and check out the court file to read the divorce awards. Divorce files are public records unless they have been sealed. Read them for yourself and find out if your attorney is telling the truth.

10. Ask your lawyer about the reputation and ability of your husband's lawyer (if he already has one). If your lawyer is not familiar with the other lawyer's capabilities, be hesitant to hire him. You know your opponent—your husband. Make sure your lawyer knows his.

## Check Out Courthouse Information
## on Lawyers

Visit with the clerks in the domestic division of your local state courthouse to obtain their recommendations on who the best divorce lawyers are. These clerks know firsthand each of the lawyers who practice domestic law. In some cases the clerks may be friends with the lawyers and will inevitably make biased recommendations. With this in mind, you should talk to several different clerks, and of course make your decision only after you have talked to the lawyer in person.

## Find Out about Judges and Their Biases

Speak with a local judge's administrative assistant to find out which lawyers the judge respects. Individuals who work within the judicial system are your best source for finding out any given lawyer's reputation.

Despite the fact that judges should ideally be impartial when presiding over a case, they do become biased in favor of or against certain lawyers and their clients. When the judge exercises his discretion to rule in one side's favor, you want to be on the side receiving the benefit of the judge's preference. Remember that the judge is only human and has the same limitations as everyone else.

Since so many of the decisions in your case are made within the judge's discretion, the better he likes your attorney, the more favorable he will be in his rulings. On the other hand, if he has a certain disdain for your lawyer, he will find little merit in your case. Worse yet, if he has a preference for your husband's lawyer, he could consistently use his power of discretion against you—and you could be in for a heap of trouble.

By carefully evaluating all the information you have collected in your search for the best lawyer, you should be able to narrow the list down to a few names. Once you have selected a lawyer, your next step is to consider how and when he will be paid for his services.

## Avoid Paying Attorney Fees Before Filing

Most lawyers perfect the fine art of overbilling immediately after leaving law school and would certainly be upset if they knew someone provided advice to their clients on how to avoid paying their fees. You may be fortunate enough to find a lawyer who will not overcharge you. More than likely, though, the lawyer you hire will milk your case for every dollar that he can possibly squeeze out of the marital estate. You will be billed for the hourly rates of your lawyer, his associate, and his paralegal, and possibly the time his secretary spent working on your case. It is not unusual for a lawyer's paralegal or secretary to be paid one hundred dollars an hour. Be wary—lawyers today are routinely sued by corporate and individual clients not only for this sort of overbilling, but for charging their clients for work which was not even performed.

In many instances, you will be able to make your husband pay for your divorce without taking any money out of your own pocket. However, any attorney worth his salt will not take your case expecting to receive his fees only from your husband, as it is not absolutely guaranteed that the court will make your husband pay for the divorce. In many cases the lawyer will end up taking a loss. Most experienced lawyers have learned to expect this loss and annually write off tens of thousands of dollars in lost fees from cases in which they represented women, the judge made the wife pay, and the wife could not afford the fees.

A lawyer figures he will usually win and obtain high fees from most cases, thus enabling him to absorb the loss from the occasional case in which the husband is not ordered to pay attorney fees. Many money-hungry lawyers even seek out women who are divorcing wealthy husbands and drive up the attorney fees astronomically, knowing that the husband will eventually end up paying them.

Ultimately though, a lawyer's greed is one that benefits the savvy woman who has learned to take advantage of it. The following case history illustrates how this can be done.

> When Paula hired her divorce lawyer, she gave him only five hundred dollars as a retainer. The lawyer, who worked for a large firm and specialized in domestic cases, realized that Paula's husband, a wealthy doctor, could easily pay his attorney fees. The lawyer agreed to obtain additional fees from the husband only after the initial retainer had been used.
>
> In planning for this lucrative case, the lawyer filed a petition for divorce and requested a huge amount of temporary alimony for Paula. To sweeten the pie, the lawyer added an additional civil suit against the husband alleging every conceivable marital tort.
>
> A tort is an injury committed against a person or property for which damages may be claimed in a court of law, and in

this case included assault and battery, marital rape, abuse, psychological duress, and many other claims.

The lawyer, his associate, paralegal, and secretary began a concerted effort to build the fees as high as possible. The lawyer charged $150 per hour, the associate charged $125 per hour, the paralegal charged $85 per hour, and the secretary charged $35 per hour, for a combined rate of $395 per hour. The divorce lawyer, certain that the court would award his fees, did not ask Paula to pay any money other than the initial $500 retainer.

The lawyer and his staff also hired an expert on battered wife syndrome and multiple local and national psychological experts for testimony on the wife's behalf. Each of these experts cost thousands of dollars, but because of his confident outlook, the lawyer spared no expense, and even spent his own money to develop the case.

At this point the amount accumulated in fees was so high that it was clear that Paula did not have the means to pay them. When the divorce trial came, the attorney spent one hour arguing that the husband should pay all of the legal expenses, but when the court finally handed down the decree of divorce, the husband was not ordered to pay the fees.

The lawyer had been unaware that this particular judge had a policy of making each side pay its own fees. Because of his oversight, he was unable to collect his fees from Paula. Ultimately, she received excellent representation, which under different circumstances would have cost her roughly one hundred thousand dollars, for a mere five hundred dollars.

As depicted in this case history, you can acquire free representation if you are skillful and lucky enough. Of course, a problem with this method is that you can be left on the hook for the payment of all fees. To avoid this, it is extremely important that you work out your fee agreement in writing with your lawyer and place a limit or cap on your personal liability. Most divorce lawyers who expect to receive most or all of their fees from the husband will agree to cap your personal liability.

If your husband has enough money in the bank, the lawyer will throw the dice much like a personal injury lawyer who represents a client on contingency fees for a percentage. Because of the ethics code of the American Bar Association and most state bar associations, divorce lawyers are not able to represent clients on contingency fees for a percentage. If your lawyer offers to do so, turn him in to the local bar association for violation of an ethics rule. Regardless of the rule on contingency fees, many divorce lawyers still treat divorce cases like personal injury lawsuits and expect to win big if their clients do.

However, this prohibition against contingent percentage attorney fees does not prevent your lawyer from agreeing to limit your liability for fees and expenses. Make sure you put the agreement in writing! An oral contract is not worth a thing.

## Find a Lawyer Who Does Not Require a Retainer

Some lawyers can be persuaded to waive a retainer if they believe your husband has substantial financial assets. You may have to look hard to find a lawyer who has not been taken advantage of by women clients who use this strategy, but if you use your feminine charm and guile, you may be able to convince some male divorce lawyers into representing you for little or nothing. The chances of finding a female lawyer who will fall for this scheme are minimal at best.

You should try to find the lawyers in your city who have big egos and represent hundreds or even thousands of women. These lawyers are the most likely to fall for your plan, as their egos often prevent them from believing that they can lose. Use this to your advantage, and keep in mind that these lawyers have hugely inflated self-images which can sometimes cloud their judgment in your favor.

When you meet with the lawyer, dress in upscale attire and look your best. Provide him with exact information on financial portfolios including stocks, real estate investments, and other monetary holdings. Once he is able to discern the amout of wealth of your husband, he will be more willing to work for a smaller amount up front. Lawyers routinely wait for their earnings.

You should speak of your husband's wealth openly and mention such things as his Mercedes, stock portfolio, yacht, or other personal property. By the time you finish, you will have this voracious lawyer drooling like a Saint Bernard over a raw T-bone steak.

## Refuse to Settle Unless He Pays Legal Fees

Make your husband pay! Make your husband pay! Make this your mantra and recite it each day until it becomes a part of your every thought. When the case gets to the point when you start talking about the property settlement, child support, and alimony, attorney fees must be included in the discussion. Use property that you know your husband wants as leverage to force him into paying your attorney fees.

When you get into the conference room to settle the case, take the opportunity to convince your husband to pay the fees. Employ the tactic of surprise. Shock your husband with your tape-recorded or other documented evidence of his misconduct (there will be more about how to acquire this evidence in later chapters). Neither he nor his lawyer can ever know whether the judge will allow this evidence of misconduct in court.

Tape-recorded evidence should never be used without proper legal advice in your own locale due to the general rule that tape-recorded evidence is inadmissible. However, several legal cases nationwide in various federal or state courts have analyzed when this type of evidence may be introduced before the court. Exceptions to the general rule of inadmissibility have been carved out. Discussion of the legal concepts involved, though, is too technical for a lay person. Because of the difficulty in determining when this type of evidence may be admitted into court, and its potential criminal implications, you must consult with a lawyer before attempting to tape record your husband on any matter related to your divorce.

To take advantage of tape-recorded evidence, you should have your lawyer request an evidentiary hearing to determine its admissibility. After the judge hears the tape, he will not be able to forget the evidence revealed on it, even if he legally rules it inadmissible. It could influence his final decision.

Once you have taken advantage of this surprise maneuver, inform your husband through your lawyer that if he pays the attorney fees you will request a year less in alimony payments. Tell him you don't need his boat or collection of cars, which you couldn't care less about. Eventually, he will cave in because he expects the court to order him to pay the fees anyway. Continue to give him small amounts of property that you know he wants until you relinquish the least amount necessary to force him to pay your fees. Only he knows what he really wants to keep, so be careful not to give him back too many of the assets with which he is willing to part.

## Squirrel Away Predivorce Savings

Just in case you cannot convince a lawyer in your city to represent you for free or very little, you must set aside money to pay a retainer and legal fees.

How much money is sufficient? Some uncontested cases can be tried for as little as a few thousand dollars, while larger cases can demand fees of over a million dollars. It depends upon two factors.

The first criterion has to do with the particular principles your lawyer may uphold. If he is an especially skilled lawyer, he can charge extremely high fees for his services. While this may seem somewhat unscrupulous, it is really just a matter of simple economic supply and demand—the more demand for the lawyer, the higher his fees become.

The second factor is the wealth of your husband and marital estate. The wealthier your husband is, the more assets there are to review and discover. Doing this requires more of the lawyer's and paralegal's time and will lead to more attorney fees.

---

*Strategy 4.*    *Save at least five thousand dollars. You may need it for your attorney.*

---

Women with upper middle class husbands should save a minimum of five thousand dollars. This amount should be sufficient to convince most lawyers to take on your initial case. Women with husbands in lower economic classes will find that a lesser amount should be sufficient. But if your husband makes over one hundred thousand dollars a year, your attorney fees could rise substantially. A good rule of thumb is to increase the amount saved for a retainer by a hundred dollars for every thousand-dollar increase in earnings above one hundred thousand dollars.

# Agree to *All* Fees with the Lawyer in Writing

Get it in writing. The importance of having your contract for attorney fees in writing cannot be reinforced enough. You need to have the lawyer specify how he bills, what he bills for, and how often he bills—in writing. Your responsibility for fees, litigation expenses, and payment for associate and clerical time should be clarified in writing so you know exactly what you are paying and for whom.

Also, if you find a lawyer who will not require a large retainer, make sure that he guarantees a cap on your liability in writing. Even today, lawyers regularly win fee disputes in ethics committees, so remember the Latin phrase "caveat emptor"— let the buyer beware!

Only the most careless lawyer will fail to document his time. A favorite lawyer's tool is to use unit billing, in which they charge minimum time fees for any task. With minimum unit billing, your case can easily reach one hundred thousand dollars in attorney fees when it should only have been ten thousand dollars.

For example, look at the following hypothetical lawyer's bill for a divorce case. The lawyer basically triples the client's bill for one month of work and charges four or five times more for his own time than he actually spends working on the case. He then doubles the charges for paralegal and secretarial time.

### Attorney Fee Bill
#### Statement for month of June 1994

| | |
|---|---|
| Phone call from client | .25 |
| Phone call from client | .25 |
| Phone call from client | .50 |
| Phone call from client | .75 |
| Phone call with accountant | 1.00 |
| Review of file | 2.50 |
| Consult with paralegal | 1.75 |
| Review of correspondence | .25 |
| Review of journal entry | .50 |
| Review of motion | .50 |
| Draft motion | 1.25 |
| Review first draft of motion | .50 |
| Review final draft of motion | .50 |
| Draft letter to client | .50 |
| Draft letter to opposing counsel | .50 |
| Review final draft of letters | .50 |

Attorney time of 12 hours
at $150.00 per hour =                    $1,800.00

Paralegal time of 20 hours
at $85.00 per hour =                        $1,700.00

Secretary time of 30 hours
at $35.00 per hour =                        $1,050.00

Total bill for June 1994 =                  $4,550.00

Reviewing the bill indicates that the twelve hours of time shown for the lawyer had actually been about two hours. Charging a minimum for the lawyer's time means that a two-minute phone call becomes fifteen minutes. The paralegal's time, which is mostly spent doing busy work, becomes just as expensive as the lawyer's. The secretary's time, which should not be billed at all, becomes an additional profit for the lawyer. Minimum unit billing has been a staple of lawyers for the past hundred years, although in recent years many suits have arisen which attack lawyers for overcharging and fraudulent billing.

To protect yourself from this chicanery, request the lawyer to state in writing that not only will no unit billing be done, but that he will be paid only for his time. He will most likely still overestimate his time, but he should bear the cost of his paralegals and secretaries. If he will not agree to these limits, do not hire him. Otherwise, you could be in for a rude awakening.

There will be a few things regarding your divorce case that you may not be able to control, but you can control your choice of lawyer and the agreements you make with him on his fees. Ethical lawyers who don't overbill their clients do exist, and perhaps you will be able to find one.

However, this quest for an honest lawyer may seem to fly in the face of your ultimate goal. On the one hand, you want the most devious, cunning lawyer money can buy, and on the other, you want a totally forthright, principled one. Decide what is more important to you and seek out the lawyer who corresponds to your needs.

# Chapter 4 | *If You've Signed a Prenuptial or Postnuptial Contract*

The single most important tool your husband can utilize to dismantle your divorce strategy is a previously signed marriage contract. Marriage contracts are normally called prenuptial or antenuptial contracts when they are signed before the marriage, and postnuptial contracts when they are signed after the marriage. In either case, the contract establishes your rights to property distribution, alimony, and other legal entitlements in the event of a divorce.

Many husbands will want you to sign not only a prenuptial contract but a postnuptial contract after the marriage to reaffirm the validity of the earlier agreement. Different jurisdictions will have varying rules concerning the validity of a prenuptial or postnuptial contract. Some courts will find that a postnuptial agreement may have significant weight in finding for the validity of the agreement, while other court systems may find directly the opposite. The important consideration for the court in either type of agreement is to determine if you were somehow fraudulently induced into signing the agreement or if there is some other legal basis for invalidating the contract. When the court makes this type of finding, you are on your way to being relieved of the terms of the contract. Your goal is to free yourself of the bonding terms of a contract of this type.

In the highly publicized divorce of Donald and Ivana Trump, for example, a marriage contract was highly contested. Ivana Trump and her bevy of lawyers challenged the contract with various legal approaches. By simply claiming that the contract was invalid on several legal grounds, Mrs. Trump's lawyers forced the opposing side to consider the possibility of losing, and thus had the necessary leverage to get Mr. Trump to pay an extra few million dollars. The legal claims may not have been strong enough to break the contract, but were compelling enough to convince Mr. Trump to pay more in the settlement rather than wait to see if the contract would be upheld in court.

The Trump divorce illustrates not only that a contract can be challenged in court, but that, ultimately, no contract is valid unless a court considers it so.

## If You Already Have Signed a Marriage Contract

Most states have adopted laws that state that a marriage contract must be favorably construed in order to be valid. What this means is that, more often, a court will try to uphold a marriage contract rather than rule it legally invalid. With this in mind, it is best to avoid being in a position which necessitates the breaching of a contract—you should refuse to sign one in the first place. If you already have signed a marriage contract, your next step is to develop a strategy for challenging it. When you want to break a marriage contract it is imperative that your lawyer look for items that were not disclosed to you at the time the agreement was signed. Looking for a loophole to break a contract can be difficult, but it can be done.

For instance, there is a law that requires the contract to be construed against the party who drafted it if any ambiguity arises in the interpretation of statements within it. In simple terms, if your husband's lawyer drafted a contract that is unclear, the court will interpret the contract in your favor. Conversely, if your lawyer drafted the contract, any ambiguities within it will be interpreted against you.

There may also be various legal loopholes that place you in an advantaged position. The less information you were provided with about your husband's financial estate before entering into the contract, the stronger your chances are for invalidating the agreement. Ask your lawyer what grounds have been found and approved by appeals courts in your state to break marriage contracts. If your contract was drafted with loopholes in mind, you stand a better chance of invalidating the contract when the time comes.

Another method that can be successful in breaking marriage contracts is to establish that the contract itself promotes divorce. Several states will invalidate the contract for this reason, because generally courts follow a public policy of attempting to preserve marriage rather than encourage divorce. When a contract is drafted to promote divorce, it does not correspond with public policy, and therefore there is less justification for the court to uphold it.

## How to Challenge a Prenuptial or Postnuptial Contract

If you have signed a contract, your next step is to develop a strategy for challenging it. Looking for a loophole to break the contract can be very difficult, but keep in mind you do have many rights in a contractual situation.

### You Signed the Contract Under False Pretenses

Claim that you and your husband entered into the contract under false pretenses by proving that you mutually agreed to it based on an inaccurate fact or set of facts. Suppose you both entered in to the contract believing that your husband would live a long and healthy life, yet unknown to both of you, he was terminally ill. Under these circumstances, neither of you would have signed the contract. But because you did enter into it under the assumption that your husband was healthy, a loophole enabling you to break the contract exists.

Another example that could enable you to break the contract would be if you entered into it believing that your husband could father a child. Perhaps, however, he is infertile and there is no chance that he can biologically reproduce. Again, in these circumstances, you have entered a marriage contract under false pretenses.

However, you must be careful about what claims you make. Following that last example, for instance, could easily lead to an annulment of the marriage. Since the marriage itself is a type of contract, your husband can use such an example to argue that the marriage was never valid and should be annulled. If the court should decide to give your husband an annulment, you could end up with nothing.

### You Were Fraudulently Induced to Sign the Marriage Contract

Another effective approach you can take to break the marriage contract is to prove that your husband had misinformed you in his attempt to convince you to sign it. If you can prove that he fraudulently induced you to sign the contract, the court will almost always invalidate it. You can do this by proving he hid assets from you.

For instance, you might show the court that at the time of marriage you were led to believe that your husband was worth only two hundred thousand dollars, but in reality, he had an oil inheritance worth ten million dollars that he had concealed from you throughout the marriage. Tell the court that you relied on your husband's supposedly truthful assertions of his worth and under this misconception had agreed to only two years of alimony at one thousand dollars a month. Explain to the court that had you known of his wealth, you would not have agreed to such a nominal sum, and that under the actual circumstances you should have been entitled to more.

### The Contract is Unfair and Unconscionable

Maybe the marriage contract is so unfair and biased in favor of your husband that you can claim it is unconscionable for the court to allow it to stand as valid. For instance, say you entered into a marriage contract that leaves you with nothing after ten or twenty years of marriage or specifies that all acquisitions obtained after the marriage belong only to your husband. Or perhaps the contract gives him custody of the children and prohibits your right to challenge that custody. In this example the contract is so egregiously unfair that there is a high probability it will be deemed unconscionable by the court.

Your contract may not be so severely unjust, but you should always claim that is unfair. Perhaps you know that your husband designed the contract so that it would benefit only him in the event that he tired of you and chose to marry someone else. Convince yourself that if he broke his promises to you, it is perfectly justifiable for you to break his contract.

### The Contract Requires You to Break the Law

Illegality in a marriage contract is difficult to prove because there must be some clause within the contract that expressly or tacitly states that unlawful conduct was required of one of the parties. Nevertheless, if you can prove that a marriage contract required you to enter into illegal conduct, you can break it. Suppose the contract legally committed you to work in your husband's business, and while doing so he demanded that you file false business records to avoid paying taxes. In this case, you can show the court that you were compelled by your husband to engage in an illegal activity in order to help him. Another, more extreme example would be one in which your husband required you to engage in his business selling illegal drugs.

### Other Loopholes

An astute lawyer will be able to determine many other legal loopholes and will challenge any contract with as many of them as possible regardless of their potential efficacy. There is no absolute assurance that a claim will be effective, so a lawyer should challenge the validity of any aspect of a marriage contract that has limited your right to receive property or alimony. Often, the threat of this challenge will be enough to get your husband to give you more than the contract specifies, as in the Trump case.

Even if the claim is entirely invalid, your husband's lawyer will have to charge him substantially to defend it. Your husband then has to consider whether it is worth his money to defend the claim or easier to give you more property in the settlement. He will also have to consider that his payment of attorney fees is not tax deductible, while his payments in alimony are. Given these two options, your husband may simply give you more in the divorce settlement.

---

*Strategy 5.*  *Challenge your prenuptial or postnuptial contract whenever you have any real basis for challenge, regardless of how small.*

---

Even if you don't win your challenge, you will at least have the satisfaction of driving up your husband's attorney fees. Remember, though—your lawyer will need to spend as much time as your husband's working on this claim. You must have a cap on your fees in order to protect yourself. If you don't, you could end up with a monumental attorney fee bill.

At the same time, beware of filing a claim which you know to have no merit, known in legalese as a "frivolous claim." Bringing such a claim may cause the judge to order your husband's fees to be paid by you, the claimant. In addition, your credibility will be damaged in all other related actions against your husband.

## Understanding the Impact of a Postnuptial Contract

As defined at the outset of this chapter, a postnuptial contract is one that is entered into after the marriage. Usually, conscientious lawyers will insist that their male clients renew this type of contract every few years so that it reflects their recent increases in wealth. Doing this gives the contract greater validity and lessens the likelihood of it being successfully challenged.

If your husband insists that you sign a postnuptial contract, make sure that it benefits you. Remember, he can't make you sign anything unless you voluntarily decide to do so. Furthermore, if your husband insists that you sign a revised postnuptial contract, remind him that you already signed one and that the one contract should be sufficient.

Chapter 5 | *Investigate and Compile Information on Your Husband's Income and Assets*

Understanding the suggestions in this chapter will be the most critical aspect of your task. Uncovering information about your husband's assets is a difficult job, and the more devious your husband is, the more arduous your assignment. Never underestimate his capabilities, regardless of how clever you may think you are. Remember, once a relationship starts falling apart, both parties begin to mask their true thoughts and schemes.

At this point, you should not trust your husband's assertions, but you should act as though you still have complete faith in him. Remain as pleasant and friendly as possible. The warmer you are with your husband the more information you can discover. If your husband begins to suspect that you are hunting for information, it could be too late. He could hide every bit of financial information in places where you may never find it.

You can assume that he has already hidden some of his financial assets from you, but once he knows you are attempting to discover the rest, he will become much like a pirate burying his booty. Even with a map, it will be difficult for you to find the treasure.

Moreover, even if your divorce lawyer is cunning, he can still be outwitted by the advice provided to your husband by his

41

lawyer. If your husband is calculating, you can expect that he hired an equally calculating lawyer, who will use all of the craftiest tactics to help his client win.

All the information found in your treasure hunt should be copied and kept in a secure storage place outside your home to prevent your husband from coming across it and discovering your plan. A good storage place would be a safe deposit box in someone else's name. Make sure, however, that you trust this person implicitly. It is best to avoid telling anyone about your arranged strategy, no matter how close you are to them. Even your closest friends can become greedy and self-serving. They may betray you in the interest of financial gain.

---

*Strategy 6.* *Never confide your plan to a relative or friend, no matter how close you are to them.*

---

Ultimately, you must be coy, alert, distrustful, and always on the lookout for new sources of information which will help you successfully enact your plan.

## Photograph *All* Personal Property

The old adage "a picture is worth a thousand words" is particularly appropriate in a divorce situation. Testimony given on the stand is subject to interpretation and differing perceptions. A photograph, however, is indisputable. For example, photographs of artwork or valuable collections that your husband possesses will be incontestable proof of his ownership, as will pictures of stock certificates made out in his name.

Be sly when obtaining photographic evidence. Take pictures of your husband at his office and be extremely careful to show him near his prized possessions. Photograph everything—household goods, artwork, vehicles, china, crystal, checkbooks, savings books, documentation of money market accounts, certificates of ownership of any asset, and all other items, documents, or objects which you believe may have value. Retain the photographs in a safe place for later use in court.

Many cases have been brought into divorce courts where a wife attempted to prove the existence of some valuable object and failed because the object vanished into thin air. Art and coin collections, rare automobiles, and other assets of substantial value can be hidden or sold for cash without traceable evidence. If this happens, the only basis for a judge's decision is your word against your husband's.

It has been said that up to eighty percent of all testimony in divorce courts is either an embellishment or an outright lie. When two people who were once in love set out to destroy each other, it is astonishing to see what lengths they will go to. Under these conditions, most divorce judges presume that people in divorce situations will lie in court.

The only way to protect yourself is to photograph or videotape your husband's assets. This way, if you testify that your husband owns a Picasso, you can bring out a photograph of it and instantly prove your claim. No further dispute need occur.

## Look for Documentation

One of the least contestable ways to prove income and assets is with written documentation. You should photocopy each and every document that you find so that it may later be admitted as evidence of your husband's additional or hidden assets. Your accountant or lawyer may also be able to use these copies to find other assets. Look for written documentation of the following items.

### Tax Returns

Your husband must file tax returns on a yearly basis. Your goal is not to analyze these tax returns, but to find and copy these documents for analysis by an accounting professional.

For example, your husband may make claims of depreciation and tax write-offs on business meals and vacations in an attempt to offset his taxable income. Depreciation is an accounting method whereby the original cost of an asset is written off over a term of years. The yearly deduction for depreciation is not an actual cash expenditure but a paper loss. In analyzing these tax documents, an accounting professional can establish which of the claimed deductions can be placed back into the income figures to project a higher income for purposes of requesting alimony and child support

Additionally, if your husband is the primary owner of a business, an accounting professional will interpret any independent records of business which may show up on his Schedule C. A Schedule C, essentially, is a profit and loss statement for tax filing purposes. If he has ownership interest in other corporations, these corporations, if not Subchapter S corporations, will typically file their own returns.

If your husband simply owns stock in a corporation and if the stock has not been sold or transferred, it will be very difficult to establish ownership from a tax record because no taxable transaction exists. His increase in wealth through stock ownership and its increase in value will not be traceable unless he is paid a dividend or other income which must be reported on his personal tax return.

*Strategy 7.* *Find and review your husband's tax returns.*

### Payroll Stubs

Obtain and keep copies of payroll stubs, which often detail retirement and profit-sharing information.

### Loan Applications and Financial Statements

When your husband is attempting to establish his net worth to obtain financing for a given business project or a loan for a personal purchase, he will most likely exaggerate his net worth. When he does so, he has signed the financial statements and loan applications under oath, thereby subjecting himself to perjury if they are found later to be untrue. You can use these signed financial statements even if they are inaccurate. He must stand by them or be subject to perjury and fraud claims in criminal and civil court. No better device exists to help you gain your fair share of his assets.

John was an oil promoter who was worth millions. Constantly needing financial assistance for his oil projects from banks, lenders, and individual investors, John became skilled in the art of creating financial statements which overestimated his oil production and made him appear more financially stable.

Because oil reserves can be evaluated in different ways, John always used the highest estimate, which boosted his apparent wealth five to ten times over his actual net worth. Furthermore, he always attempted to make a particular oil project more appealing by making his company look more profitable than it actually was so investors would finance his deals. At the same time, he looked for every possible tax deduction so that it would appear he was losing money on his tax returns. After his wife initiated divorce proceedings against him, he systematically concealed or destroyed all written evidence of oil prospectuses on his various companies so that they would not be subject to discovery in court. By the time his wife's lawyers were able to secure any documents, all they could find were tax returns and a few loan documents. Because of this inability to find the pertinent documents, the wife agreed to settle out of court for hundreds of thousands of dollars less than she was actually entitled to. Had she understood more about her husband's finances, she could have photocopied the prospectuses, financial statements, and loan applications, all of which overstated his net worth and income. Unfortunately, she was only able to establish his taxable income, which had been greatly reduced by every possible legal deduction. In this particular divorce war, the wife lost by a substantial amount.

---

*Strategy 8.*   *To win in court, you must have evidence. Copy every bit of financial evidence about your husband's assets that you can locate.*

---

# How and Where to Find Your Husband's Assets

Unearthing your husband's hidden assets can be a challenging task. There are various ways to accomplish this mission, some more difficult than others. For example, stock certificates, bonds, bank books, and monthly or quarterly statements will be the easiest for your husband to conceal, because generally the only evidence of these assets are the actual documents themselves. If these documents are kept in a safe-deposit box under a company name and statements are mailed to a post office box, you may not be aware of them or able to find them. However, your husband may have some type of documented evidence of these holdings in his office in order to have the relevant information on hand for loan applications and financial statements. You can casually drop by his place of work and tell his secretary that you are there to drop off a gift. There, in his office, you may be able to find this evidence.

Furthermore, if a financial asset pays interest, the interest payer will send out a tax statement on which the government will tax interest. The income from this interest will be disclosed on his year-end tax return, but possibly in a different earnings category. If, on the other hand, there is absolutely no interest and the certificate of ownership is the only proof of the asset, you should find out who your husband's stockbroker is and get to know him or her. You may be able to obtain valuable information.

Remember, proof may not be readily apparent. Your husband's financial holdings can be elaborately concealed not only from you, but from the IRS and creditors. Look thoroughly and carefully—each discovery will lead to another, perhaps more deviously hidden asset. The following sections of the chapter will advise you on how to accomplish this.

## Visit the Bank Safe-Deposit Box

In general, you cannot access another person's safe deposit box legally unless your name and signature are on file with the depository. Unauthorized access could conceivably constitute criminal activity in some jurisdictions. If your husband has a safe deposit box that you don't have legal access to, consult with your attorney on how to proceed. You may be able to access the safe-deposit box after obtaining a court order. Keep in mind, however, that if your husband knows that you are on the hunt for his assets, he will not only remove evidence of them from the box, but quickly take steps to conceal all other evidence.

## Review Bank and Credit Card Receipts

Time-consuming and tedious as it is, reviewing your husband's checkbook, cancelled checks, and deposit slips will be necessary in order to thoroughly investigate his assets. In most instances, if your husband made a substantial deposit, it will either have come from his salary or the sale of an asset. By tracing deposits, you can establish a table in which you can chart them against assumed earnings. Create a flow chart with a record of the dates and amounts of the deposits, and if obtainable, the stated source. Doing this will allow you to determine if the deposits are routine transactions from earnings or occasional random deposits which reflect the sale or transfer of assets.

Cancelled checks will enable you to determine purchases and transfers. If your husband has other accounts which you are not aware of, transfers to other banks or financial institutions will help you find them. Payments made by check for fees to brokers, accountants, or lawyers can also be delved into to garner proof of earnings and holdings.

If your husband has many accounts, he may keep business checks for many corporate entities that will not be traceable through this method. In order to be certain that you have indeed located all of the possible transfer locations, you must have all of the checks. However, it may be impossible to locate all of these checks without having a lawyer submit written interrogatories and requests for your husband to respond in writing, under oath, as to the location of all potential assets.

*Strategy 9.*    *Checks and deposit slips tell a story about your husband that you never knew.*

Credit card receipts tell another story. These receipts will be useful in tracking all of your husband's credit card purchases and will establish his various credit sources. If you compile a complete list of all credit accounts, your lawyer can obtain the financial statements your husband submitted to obtain credit. The statements may project a level of earnings on an annual basis. However, because each statement is different, some may be more informative than others.

Credit card receipts will also indicate where he spends his free time and money when you are not around. Reviewing them will tell you the following:

1. Where he eats and drinks when you are not with him.
2. Which hotels and motels he has visited without you.
3. Whether he has been a customer at ladies' clothing boutiques or perfume shops to purchase items for another woman.
4. Whether he visits escort services, strip clubs, and other men's establishments without your knowledge.
5. Whether he has bought jewelry for another woman.
6. Whether his "business trip" was to Chicago or to the Bahamas with another woman.

Credit cards bills may be paid from checking accounts kept at your husband's office. If your husband receives his credit card statements at his office where you can't review them, he is probably hiding something from you.

## Befriend Stockbrokers and Secretaries

Establishing personal relationships with your husband's stockbroker and secretary will present you with many opportunities to acquire information about your husband's financial situation. Chat with them so that they become comfortable with you on an informal basis. If you form a congenial rapport with them, you can catch them off-guard. They may reveal some pertinent details which will help you in your search.

Place an occasional call to your husband's stockbroker under the pretense that you are inquiring into your husband's various holdings on his behalf. You can tell the stockbroker that your husband requested you to call and get information for his CPA or financial advisor. If the broker has not been previously warned by your husband to withhold this information, you will be able to obtain this valuable knowledge.

Your husband's secretary is another important source of information. A truly busy husband will not have the time to keep all of his finances in line and will usually trust someone else with this duty. Often this person is his secretary. Keep in mind that most men will reveal more financial information to their secretaries than to their wives.

If you become close enough to his secretary, she will unwittingly furnish you with much-needed insight into his financial dealings. In most cases, this disloyalty to her employer will not be intentional—the disclosure will occur almost naturally if you are shrewd enough.

It will be up to you to develop a friendship with his secretary to earn her trust. Friends help friends. She may never realize that by disclosing confidential information she breached your husband's trust.

Also, don't forget to become friendly with the secretaries of his business associates, brokers, financial advisors, and lawyers. Many women will stick together to help one another in a time of need. With the promise of ultimate confidence, you can detect many clandestine business deals without your husband ever learning about any breach in confidentiality.

Once you earn the trust of these other people, you will have to determine if their confidence can be assured. If one of these secretaries has lost her own divorce case, her sympathies may lie with you. However, you can only learn this by becoming and remaining friendly with these women. Over time, you will learn as much as you would like—or more.

When talking to your husband's business associate or secretary, an effective tactic is to persuade the person that you urgently need to help your husband. Convince them that, because of this urgency, you need the information as quickly as possible. This technique will often throw them off-guard long enough for you to obtain the data. Be careful, though; this technique may expose your search.

---

*Strategy 10.* *Be clever and shrewd. Ask the right questions and be friendly with all of your husband's financial advisors, stockbrokers, attorneys, and secretaries.*

---

# Photocopy Business Telephone Records

Phone records are another good source of evidence, as they will inform you of long-distance calls made from your husband's place of business. If monies are being kept in offshore bank accounts, he will need to speak with his banker or advisor and inquire about these accounts from time to time. If you have the phone records, you can call any suspicious numbers listed on them to determine whom your husband was calling.

Out-of-state property holdings require management, as does ownership of corporations or interest in other businesses. Tracing out-of-state phone calls can lead to the discovery of these entities, which can be another considerable advantage in the divorce war.

Also remember to check telephone calls made on your husband's mobile phone. He may use a calling card that you are not aware of, so you will need to find out the credit card company and number. Once the divorce suit has been filed, your lawyer will be able to use this information to find out more about your husband's financial situation.

While reviewing phone records may seem dull and boring, the time you spend doing this may lead to your discovery of significant assets. Isn't the time and effort worth the potential gain?

# Trace Financial Statements—Backwards

If you are not a number cruncher or math whiz, reviewing financial statements may be of no benefit to you. Nevertheless, you should know the rationale behind obtaining the documentation. It is imperative to use these documents to trace backwards in the financial search.

Tracing backwards means you look at an income indicated on a financial statement and trace the source of that income. Even the most minute bit of income data can lead to a larger source of earnings.

While searching backwards, it becomes important to look for notations referring to other assets. An example would be the financial disclosure indicated in a financial statement reflecting ownership of corporate stock. One such disclosure can lead to indications of financial wealth.

Assume, for example, that the disclosure of corporate ownership of stock reveals that your husband is on the directorial board of a company you were not aware of. Perhaps he is withholding the receipt of income and stock dividends until the divorce has been finalized. If you don't find out about it before the divorce is granted, you could be prevented from receiving your share of this asset.

If your husband is in the middle class, a different example is in order. His employer may have provided him with various types of retirement plans or profit sharing plans at work. Some of these might not have any real taxable effect until he would cash them in.

Most employers will provide an employee handbook or manual. These documents may disclose the types of fringe benefits provided to company employees that your husband forgot to tell you about.

# Investigate Your Husband's Income and Assets

Susan was married for a long time and was a loving wife and devoted mother. However, when she discovered that her husband was having an affair with his secretary, she filed for divorce. Unbeknownst to Susan, the husband, who worked as retail merchant in an expensive jewelry store, had secretly become a silent partner in the business. This partnership had been concealed because of the affair with the secretary, which had been going on for some time.

The other business partner had contractually agreed to transfer fifty percent of the business to Susan's husband contingent upon on his services and a twenty percent weekly holdback from his salary. This holdback could not be traced because it was not disclosed anywhere except in the secret contract between the two partners. One mistake, however, led to the discovery of this silent transaction.

As part of the partnership arrangement, Susan's husband was required to cosign a business line of credit. The money held back from his salary had been placed in an interest-bearing account that was held in both parties' names as collateral for the line of credit in the event of default. In applying for this line of credit, Susan's husband wrote down his ownership of these secret funds. Over a period of one year, $50,000 in marital assets, which Susan was entitled to, had been placed into this account.

The ownership of the business was due to be transferred six months after the divorce was finalized. At the time Susan found a copy of the application for the line of credit, the store had been valued by an appraiser at a net worth of $750,000, half of which belonged to Susan's husband. Susan's discovery of one seemingly insignificant statement entitled her to make a claim for half of the $50,000 in the secret account and half of the husband's ownership of the jewelry store.

Needless to say, Susan's discovery of her husband's financial statements was crucial to her case. Don't overlook this important avenue in your divorce.

Finally, place yourself in your husband's shoes at the moment he first learns of the imminent divorce. He will make phone calls to his stockbroker, CPA, and financial advisor that will quickly start the chain of deceit. From this point on, your husband will be obsessed with the quest to hide his assets and defray the potential losses which your plan of attack may cause. He, too, will establish a sophisticated strategy to win the divorce war. But remember, nothing hurts a man more than losing his money. Once you know the love is gone, you can retaliate for all the pain he caused you by digging into his wallet.

Regardless of the techniques, procedures, and advice presented in this book, much of your husband's assets can still be hidden with the help of competent counsel. The only possible defense against this chicanery is to hire the most crafty and cunning lawyer in your area. You need to hire a lawyer who likes to dig for buried treasure. And keep in mind—once the decision to divorce has been made, you will immediately be in a race to the courthouse. Ultimately, the winner of the race will be the faster, more knowledgeable party. No one wants to play this game, but once you have entered it, it is too late.

*Strategy 11.* *The first person to make it to the courthouse has the better chance of winning the divorce war.*

# Chapter 6 | *Begin to Hide Money and Purchase Assets*

An important factor in a successful divorce is your ability to accumulate cash for the rehabilitation period following the legal suit. No matter how much you are awarded for alimony or child support in the temporary orders of your divorce, it will most likely not be enough to sustain you. You want to walk away from the marriage in a financial position equal to your husband's.

Your subsequent financial status will determine your standard of living, who you will be able to socialize with, and how long after the divorce you will be able to remain financially stable. The more cushion you can build for the lean months after the divorce, the happier you will be.

---

**Strategy 12.** *You must build a financial cushion prior to filing for divorce so you will not suffer during and following your divorce.*

---

## Cash Checks at Grocery Stores

One of the better methods of obtaining cash is to write checks for groceries from joint or single checking accounts. This method is easy to enact and will not arouse a great degree of suspicion. If you cook an occasional dish of oysters Rockefeller or shrimp scampi, your husband will be convinced the grocery money is being well spent. If your husband places complete trust in you, he will not scrutinize the amounts of money you spend on seemingly valid purchases.

> Mary, who was married to a wealthy man, established a routine of cashing checks before filing for divorce. However, her husband, who intricately charted the couple's banking accounts, noticed a pattern of abnormal spending. He noticed that she would go to three or four grocery stores on one day, writing checks for even sums which clearly did not reflect sales taxes or odd amounts as a normal grocery bill would. Her husband correctly assumed that Mary's intent in writing these checks was to obtain cash. Nevertheless, despite his detection, Mary's plan worked perfectly. The court found no merit in the husband's arguments at trial. Ultimately, the fact that the husband could establish a withdrawal pattern of thousands of dollars did not make any difference to the court because of his wealth. In other words, regardless of the detectable, provable withdrawal of funds planned for divorce, the court chose to favor the wife.
>
> Remember, though, that not all judges think alike. They act upon their own individual intuition and discretion. With this in mind, spread the days out in which you write checks and stagger them throughout the week at different food chains or other merchants who will cash your checks. The more diverse your record of checks is, the less your chance of being detected.

## Use Cash Advances on Credit Cards

If there are credit cards in your husband's name that you can sign, you have another easy vehicle to build up predivorce assets. However, with this method, you must be much more crafty, because each withdrawal will produce a record of credit receipts that cannot be hidden. You must establish valid reasons for the cash advances. Some reasonable grounds for withdrawing a cash advance are suggested below, but as long as the justifications you develop appear viable to the court, your plan will probably succeed.

Some generally valid reasons for cash advances are:

1. You needed to have extra cash to buy groceries.
2. You needed extra cash to buy a present for him.
3. You needed cash to buy relatives necessary items for living. (You know your relatives will back you up. You were embarrassed to ask him.)
4. He would not provide you enough living expense money and you needed to take additional funds to buy necessary items for the home.
5. You needed the money for clothes or shoes because he would not let you buy any.

There are a thousand reasons for borrowing money against the credit cards which will be acceptable in the court's estimation. Coming up with these reasons and getting the money out of the credit accounts before the court orders your husband to pay the bill should be your goal.

The plan *could* backfire on you in the event that a court determines you were removing marital assets from the marital estate rather than spending the advances on necessary living expenses. In that event, you might have the court find you responsible for the amount advanced. The court would then offset your claim to the marital estate by a similar amount or make you pay the funds back to the marital estate for division by the court between you and your husband.

Another major problem with this plan is the discretion of the court. It is possible that the court will decide you are responsible for building up the credit card balances and therefore should pay the debt. Perhaps the court might decide you are unable to pay the debt, in which case it may take the total balances owed and offset them against money your husband would have given you in a property distribution. In short, when you carry out a plan with a suspicious motive, don't always expect to be rewarded—you could end up with less than you would have otherwise received.

The more clever your reasoning for the withdrawal, the higher the probability that you will be relieved of the debt obligation. Remember that if a card is in your name, none of the above reasoning applies, as it is likely that the court will order you to pay your own credit card debt.

## Take Out Cash from Checking and Savings Accounts

In many divorces, a wife is advised by her lawyer to empty the marital bank accounts during the period prior to filing for divorce. No competent lawyer will ever admit under oath that they told a client to do this, but it is an everyday occurrence.

A lawyer will make this recommendation because when temporary orders are in place, all assets can be frozen, and you may be restricted from removing funds from the accounts. Typically, the court will entitle one party to receive funds from an account while restricting the other. Worse yet, the accounts can be frozen entirely.

In many instances, the court may not hold the preliminary withdrawal of funds against you. But you should realize that the opposite can occur. The court may rule that this money is subject to division and hold it against the future distribution of marital property as an offset for your misconduct. It is up to you to decide whether it is worth the risk.

## Begin to Hide Money and Purchase Assets

You can build up a bevy of reasons for withdrawing the cash that will allow the court to disregard your actions. Your lawyer will be able to assist you in determining several valid needs for the money, but one of the most convincing is the payment of an attorney fee retainer for your lawyer. Since the judge is a lawyer, he or she can easily sympathize with this reason.

Following are other valid reasons that can be shown.

1.  Money needed for a deposit on a rental home or apartment, including the first few months' rent.
2.  Money to pay bills owed such as car payments, credit cards, and other installment loans.
3.  Moving expenses.
4.  New furniture purchases for a separate household.
5.  New appliances and other necessary items for the home.

Make the expenditure appear as a necessary living expense. This will generally be recognized as a valid reason for retention of the funds without the court offsetting it against the distribution of marital assets.

---

*Strategy 13.* *Always determine valid reasons why you had to withdraw cash from a joint or individual account to prevent the court from ordering you to give the money back.*

---

In most instances, the spending of money from a joint or individual account seems to be such a trivial matter in the court's assessment that it will not inquire into the taking of the funds as long as some valid reason can be stated for the withdrawal.

Furthermore, never leave funds in bank accounts for your husband's use if you can validly access them in the predivorce stage. Just as the person who files for divorce first stands in a better position to fight the divorce, the party going to trial with the most cash has the greater leverage.

# Before Divorce, Buy Assets You Can Take with You after Separation

If you are seeking a divorce, it is likely that your life has become dull and tedious. Predivorce acquisition of assets can provide daily amusement which will alleviate your boredom until the divorce has been finalized and you have the freedom to pursue a new life. Once you have this freedom, you can find Mr. Right and have the life you have always yearned for, but in the meantime you might as well have some fun.

While preparing for your divorce, you should not overlook the acquisition of additional personal property which you may be able to keep after the divorce without having to pay back your husband. Judges overlook, or sometimes ignore, predivorce spending on assets. In a majority of divorce suits, they award personal property purchased by one party before the divorce to that party and not to their spouse. This is not always the case, but it happens often enough to pursue. This potential judicial oversight provides you with an additional opportunity to obtain more assets for your postdivorce period.

The potential worst-case scenario is one of two things. Either you will be allowed to retain the property and your husband will be allowed an offset against payments to you, or he will be allowed to retain the property. If you are a gambler at heart, then gamble away to your heart's content.

Whether you are allowed to keep all of the property you purchase for yourself may depend upon whether you are in a community property state or an equitable distribution state. The difference can be substantial.

### In Community Property States

Community property states, the largest of which is California, have divorce laws which generally provide that assets acquired during the marriage will be evenly divided between the parties at the time of divorce. (See Appendix A for a listing of the states with community property laws.) However, the community property law can be radically altered by a marriage contract, which will impair your ability to obtain marital assets.

The community property rationale provides a basis for you to receive half of everything you or your husband purchases during the marriage. If you purchase cars, stocks, IRAs, bank savings accounts, boats, or any other assets together, you can claim half. If one party purchases the property during the marriage, you have a valid basis to state a claim for one-half of the property or one-half of the value. For women, a community property state is ideal.

In a community property state, it is conceivable your husband will be awarded half of everything you purchase in the period immediately prior to the divorce, but you can avoid this by purchasing assets for yourself that he will not like. Buy women's clothing, jewelry, or other typically feminine articles. Decorate the house with new furnishings in styles and colors that are distasteful to your husband. Is he really going to want the new pink leather couch after the divorce? During the marriage he will have acquiesced to your preferences, but he won't want the property you purchased once he is a bachelor.

If you did not get married in a community property state but can convince your husband to move to a state with community property laws, you can obtain a divorce under the same theory. The benefits of residing in a community property state are considerable.

Keep in mind that all jurisdictions have residency requirements to file for divorce, and you may have to reside for a substantial period of time in the second jurisdiction in advance of filing for divorce. Consult with your attorney for more information on the laws in your area.

### In Equitable Distribution States

Equitable distribution states do not necessarily award half of whatever was acquired during the marriage to you. In an equitable distribution state the court will review assets acquired before and after the marriage, and can look at property to be inherited. Based upon the particular elements of the case, a court can award property and assets to either party.

The court will look at factors such as the following:

1. The record of ownership of the property.
2. Whether the property was acquired before the marriage.
3. Whether the property was acquired as a gift, or as an inheritance from a relative.
4. How long the property was owned.
5. The fault of the parties.
6. The age of the parties.
7. The length of the marriage.
8. The property owned by the parties.
9. The present and future earning capacities of the parties.
10. The time, source, and manner of acquisition of the property.
11. The family ties and obligations related to the property.
12. The determination of allowance of alimony or maintenance to a spouse.
13. The dissipation or wasting of assets by one party.

These factors are but a few of the many that courts will review to determine what a party will receive in a settlement.

Each state may have a different standard of review, and an individual court may look at some or all of the listed factors. A lawyer specializing in matrimonial law in your area can best discuss what factors the local courts use to award property.

> Jan entered into a loveless marriage for the sole purpose of acquiring money. She had been married to her husband for only six months when the relationship began to lapse into a state of hatred, distrust, and general ill-will. Prior to the marriage, her husband, a wealthy doctor with a large medical practice, was earning four to five hundred thousand dollars a year, while Jan was earning only ten to fifteen thousand a year.
>
> Upon filing for divorce, she lied and overstated her husband's income in order to get a temporary alimony award of ten thousand dollars per month. Her husband then successfully filed a motion to reduce the award because of her fraudulent claim. Furthermore, when the divorce came to trial, Jan's husband presented evidence that she had attempted to blackmail him by threatening to disclose his various marital indiscretions to the Board of Professional Regulation for doctors. These indiscretions included smoking marijuana, going to topless bars, and sleeping with a patient.
>
> When the judge considered this evidence, he readily believed it in view of the fraudulent claim Jan had made previously. After a long trial and lengthy closing statements, the judge only awarded Jan nine hundred dollars in alimony for a period of three months. Additionally, he ordered her to return artwork and valuables which her husband owned prior to the marriage and Jan had since removed from the house.
>
> Finally, the judge not only ordered Jan to pay all of her debts and credit obligations, but demanded that she pay her own attorney fees even though he knew the husband could afford them. Ultimately, because Jan failed to accurately evaluate her husband's financial situation and did not approach her divorce with the necessary shrewdness, she walked away from the marriage with a large debt. She was even forced to sell her new sports car because she was unemployed and could not afford the payments on it.

The most important lesson learned here is that being too vicious can backfire. Jan's attempt to use blackmail was wrong.

The end result was her ultimate loss in the divorce. Blackmail can never be advocated.

This case history presents several useful strategies which you should remember for your divorce.

---

*Strategy 14.* *Never perpetrate a fraud upon the court, or your best-laid plans will backfire.*

---

---

*Strategy 15.* *Use accurate financial records during divorce proceedings so the court will award the proper temporary and permanent alimony.*

---

---

*Strategy 16.* *Never make a blackmail attempt upon your husband. A judge can hold this against you in the final award of property.*

---

In an equitable distribution state, the circumstances must be favorable for you to retain possession of a predivorce asset. If you can present compelling reasons or justifications for a purchase, the chances that a court will allow you to keep your personal property are greater.

For example, by showing the court the asset was purchased for your birthday or Valentine's Day, you will most likely be able to retain it because judges in equitable distribution states generally lean toward awarding property to the party who received it as a gift. Or perhaps your husband was caught in an affair and told you to redecorate the house. Maybe he bought a new car and allowed you to pick out one at the same time. He may have made an agreement with you allowing you to buy property and keep it for yourself in the event of a divorce because he felt guilty over some infidelity.

If you received a card signed by your husband with the gift, retain it for evidence to prove to the judge you are telling the truth. Record relevant information in a daily diary so you can introduce it as evidence to show your husband's intention at the time of the purchase. Your ability to creatively develop reasons for the purchase of an asset will ultimately benefit you when the time comes for a judge to allocate your mutually or personally owned possessions.

## Redecorate the House with New Furniture

If your lawyer feels you have a high likelihood of being awarded the house, it will behoove you to do some remodeling before filing for divorce. Replace the carpets, drapes, and cabinets, and update all the appliances. Install a pool, hot tub, and Jacuzzi. Elaborately decorate the house. All of the money you spend on redecorating your home will most likely be disregarded as an improvement of a mutual marital asset.

More often than not, a court will order the home to be sold with the equity split among the parties. If you have young children, your lawyer can argue that they should not be removed from the home. This argument may allow you to stay in the home until they reach age eighteen, whereupon the home will be sold with the equity divided. Until then, you will be able to enjoy all of your improvements.

Do not take out a mortgage or other loan to pay for the remodeling. You might end up with the bill for the second mortgage, which will reduce the spendable income from your alimony award. Only spend what you can pay for from your husband's salary and savings.

The larger the expenditures, the better off you will be after the divorce. Your husband may think he is helping to keep the marriage intact by paying for these improvements. For you, however, these expenditures are an additional prize for your future.

Remember, in most instances, judges fail to take into consideration expenditures on home redecoration. Do it and do it right. You can have that magnificent house all to yourself.

## Purchase a New Car Just Before Divorce

Another wonderful way to obtain an asset for yourself is to acquire a new car. Be certain that your husband pays for the car in cash, as a loan payment may end up being your responsibility. If you both purchase new cars, however, there is no reason that the court will not award each of you your own vehicle.

Be careful what you choose. Buy a car with a high resale value. After the divorce you might need to turn the car into cash for living expenses. Stick with imports, such as Mercedes Benz, BMW, Porsche, and other expensive vehicles that are easy to sell. If you buy a car that has a high enough value, you can sell the car after the divorce and still purchase a vehicle that meets your standards.

## Trade in Old Assets for New Assets

Trading assets applies to any kind of property, regardless of whether it is personal property, real estate, bank accounts, or stocks. Create a list of all of your marital property. Determine which property you no longer like. Convince your husband to sell or trade it for new property.

Take the example where your furniture is old and worn out after two or three years. You have your eye on this new Italian living room set. Buy it for the house. Pay cash for it. If you can arrange for the property to be bought as a gift for you for Christmas, your birthday, Valentine's Day, or some other special occasion, then do it. In community property states you are entitled to half of the property by law, so you can't possibly lose. This is just another reason why you want to be divorced in a community property state whenever possible.

Another example of trading up property is the instance where you have kitchen appliances or a washer and dryer. You, of course, want the new designer models. Your toilet fixtures are white and you want a designer color. Purchase the expensive models to replace the old boring look. It will make you happier when you have your beautiful home with its sparkling new kitchen to convince your next husband that you are a wonderful housewife.

The only limitation to this analysis is your imagination. Make everything new and beautiful while you have the opportunity, the money, and the ability. In the postdivorce period, your assets and disposable income will become limited. Remember, forget the foregoing advice on predivorce acquisition if your lawyer does not believe you have a fair chance of receiving the home. Predivorce spending should then be concentrated on cars, clothing, furs, jewelry, and other items of property not related to the home.

# Set up IRAs and Retirement Accounts in Your Name

Convince your husband to open a retirement account or other savings account in your name only. Have him make routine payments to the account to build it up to a sizable investment as he sets up his own accounts at the same time. The court will be able to look at the fairness of awarding you your individual cash accounts if your husband has his own. While making improvements to your asset position, always spend the money from his accounts and save your funds. If you can show the court that equal amounts were placed into each spouse's accounts and that you were careful in saving yours while your husband was not, there is a great probability the court will allow you to retain the entire balance of your account.

In a community property state, the court may simply divide the amounts saved, which leads to another strategy.

---

*Strategy 17.* *The more you and your husband save, the more you get in the divorce trial.*

---

The foregoing analysis is not based simply upon bank and savings accounts. The procedures can be used to build up stock portfolios, money market accounts, mutual funds, and any other investment accounts which will benefit you.

Whenever you purchase a stock, bond, or fund, make sure your husband receives an equal amount. It should not concern you if he is left with an asset after your divorce, so long as you are allowed to retain all of the funds that are in your name.

# Chapter 7 | *Stay or Be Unemployed Before Divorce*

In seeking an award for alimony or maintenance, your employability is a huge factor. If you have been working for a long time before you file for divorce, it is not wise to simply quit your job and expect the judge to believe you should receive alimony. The judicial system will consider the voluntary termination from your job as an obvious attempt to acquire alimony, and will most likely disregard or minimize your unemployed status if it appears to have been strategically planned.

Maximization is the key to living better after the divorce. You want the judge to believe that you are genuinely unemployable, and therefore entitled to the maximum alimony award.

If you are a housewife who has not worked for years, you are in a much better position than your employed counterpart. The longer the period of unemployment, the more favorable the court will be. An award of alimony will be higher in amount and longer in length when you have been unemployed for a long period.

***Strategy 18.*** *Be unemployed for as long a period of time as possible prior to filing for divorce.*

Strategy is crucial. You must convince the court that your unemployment and unemployability are based upon valid circumstances. You must project the attitude that you want to be employed, but because of these circumstances are simply unable to obtain employment. Only you know for sure why you are unemployable.

## How Long Should You Be Unemployed?

The length of your unemployment period is highly important. In most cases, longer unemployability results in a longer receipt of alimony. At the very least, you should attempt to be unemployed for a year prior to filing for divorce. If you quit your job or are fired and then three months later file for divorce, the court will assume that you will return to work in a short period of time. In this case, an award of rehabilitative alimony for a period of six months to a year might be in order. You will probably feel this is not enough retribution against your husband, and certainly is not long enough to enjoy the fruits of your labor. It may hardly be worth going through with the divorce if you are going to receive alimony for only a year or less.

On the other hand, take the following hypothetical situation. You have been unemployed for two to three years and your husband has a job as vice president of sales for a manufacturing company and earns eighty thousand dollars per year in addition to bonuses and expenses. You have raised his children and been with him for twenty years. During this time your husband requested that you not attend college, because he wanted you to raise his children properly. You were therefore unable to acquire any real specialized skills. Most of your work experience has been in retail sales or some other area that helped to take up time, but did not provide the family with any significant additional income. With tough economic times, you have been unable to get another job because of your lack of marketable job skills.

In this instance, the court will look favorably upon your position. You have devoted most of your life to your husband, helped raise the family, and made many sacrifices. During this same period of time, your husband has been educated. He has progressed through job promotion and change to the high position in life he now holds, and at this point, you can not possibly catch up with him. Fairness dictates that you should be placed on equal footing with him in the postdivorce period. Only one thing will accomplish this—an award of alimony for a long period of time at a fairly hefty monthly amount.

You can see by this analysis how important the length of time and justifications for unemployability are. The following two case histories, with differing outcomes, will help you to further understand the manner in which a court determines alimony based on unemployment.

Molly was married to her husband for only four years. Her husband worked as a stockbroker and earned an income of approximately one hundred twenty thousand dollars a year. Molly was thirty-four years old at the time of the divorce, and her husband was forty.

When the two were first married, Molly had been working as a secretary earning eighteen thousand dollars a year. She remained employed during the whole marriage until she was fired just two months before filing for divorce. Neither Molly's husband nor the court knew she had conjured the situation which ultimately led to her termination so that she could claim alimony.

No unusual factors appeared in this divorce which were in her favor other than her unemployment. The court looked objectively at the factors involved in the case and ordered Molly's husband to pay alimony for nine months in the amount of one thousand dollars per month. A significant factor in the court's decision to grant this relatively nominal alimony award was Molly's experience as a secretary both before and after the marriage. Under these circumstances it was apparent that her unemployability would only be temporary. As soon as she found another job, she would be back in the same position she was in prior to the marriage.

Judy was married for seven years before filing for divorce. Both she and her husband were in their forties. Her husband was an orthodontist making slightly over one hundred thousand dollars a year.

Judy had three children during the marriage. From the outset of the marriage, her husband insisted that she not work so she could be at home to raise the family. Prior to the marriage Judy had been employed as an airline hostess, and although she had been in the airline business for years, this was her only experience. She had attended college for one year but did not earn a degree. Also, Judy had sold her condominium right after they were married and used the equity, ten thousand dollars, toward a down payment on their house, while her husband contributed forty thousand dollars.

Not long after the birth of their second child, Judy's husband began to have an affair that continued until the time of the divorce. With three children to take care of, Judy won the sympathy of the court. Her only skills were as an airline hostess, and because the economy had changed there were few prospects for employment in the airline industry. The children needed either their mother or a full-time baby sitter.

The court awarded the house to Judy because the children needed to be in a stable, familiar environment. To help make the house payments, the court awarded Judy not only a large amount of monthly child support, but also two thousand dollars a month in alimony until the youngest child reached age eighteen.

Certainly, there is quite a contrast between these two case histories. Judy's case obviously presented stronger arguments for a substantial long-term alimony award. The courts can go either way depending upon hundreds, perhaps thousands, of variables. This means that you must structure the case in your favor by placing as many factors in your corner as possible.

# How to Leave Your Job Legitimately

Convincing a court you have left your job for a valid reason is harder than you may think. Many trivial reasons for leaving your employment can be shown, so it is important that you present factual, compelling justifications. If you cannot show a substantial reason for leaving your job, you should simply move on to another aspect of your divorce plan. Most judges are savvy enough to distinguish valid reasons for unemployment from deceit and trickery—they are accustomed to hearing thousands of lies and variations on similar lies. You need to be astute when formulating your reasons for leaving your job.

---

*Strategy 19.* *The longer you are unemployed before filing for divorce, the better your chances are of receiving long-term alimony.*

---

Some, but certainly not all, valid reasons for leaving your job are listed below.

1. Termination from your job. No better reason can be presented. Watch out, though—if you were intentionally trying to get fired, your husband can get your past employer to corroborate this.

2. Layoff from your job. A layoff from a job will provide an excellent basis for convincing the judge you are validly unemployed.

3. Quitting work to take care of your children. This is a tricky one. Why do they need you at home? If your children are past elementary school age and do not have special needs, this may not work for you.

4. Quitting work at your husband's request, which can be proven in writing, by witnesses, or by tape-recorded evidence. When you can submit evidence to the court that your husband requested you to quit work, you have a good chance of receiving a better alimony award. However, proving that your husband required you to quit work is difficult, if not impossible, without out hard physical evidence.

5. Quitting work to care for a sick relative. While this is a valid reason, if the relative is not a member of your immediate family, the court may find little merit in it.

6. Quitting work to obtain a formal education to match the education of your husband. If you put your husband through college and he promised to send you to college after he became financially established or after the children were out of high school, a very strong argument can be made in your favor.

7. Quitting work to perform work-related tasks for your husband's business. Many husbands become dependent upon their wives' help in their business. Did he ask you to give up your job as an administrative assistant or teacher to help make his business more profitable? If he did, were you paid wages, or did he fail to pay you wages and thereby fail to set up a base of earnings for your right to claim Social Security later on in life? Now your only job skills are for his business. You have no true earnings history. The judge should consider this in your favor.

There may be hundreds of other valid reasons to leave your employment. Those just listed are valid reasons routinely viewed by courts as justifications to quit your employment.

## Create Reasons for Unemployment and Alimony

The preceding section revealed valid reasons for quitting your job. This section gives valid reasons to remain unemployed after the marriage, thereby entitling you to long-term alimony.

Proving to the court that you will remain unemployable in the future for any definite period of time is much more difficult than establishing a justification for short-term unemployability.

You must convince the court that you are unemployable now and will be for as long a period as possible. The longer the period of time, the better.

Your ultimate goal should be to obtain lifetime alimony payments. If you do, remember that courts usually structure lifetime or long-term alimony payments with contingencies. This means that if a particular event occurs, the court will terminate the alimony. Those events most frequently cited by a court are:

1.  Death.
2.  Remarriage.
3.  Cohabitation with a member of the opposite sex who is not a member of your family.

In some circumstances, the court or your husband can be convinced to take one or all of these contingencies out of the order of alimony. You must strive for an order with no contingencies, or as few as possible. When one of the contingent events occurs, you lose and your husband wins.

## Valid Reasons for Remaining Unemployed

The list below provides some, but not all, potential reasons why you are likely to remain unemployed. Ingenuity and creativity will allow you to expand the list almost infinitely.

1.  Your present age. Age is probably the single most important criterion. The older you are, the less chance you have of finding employment.
2.  Lack of education. If you have only a high school diploma or minimal college education, you can present a much stronger case for your inability to find suitable employment.

3.  Unemployability due to lack of skill. If your husband
    has requested that you not work for most of your mar-
    ried life or refused to allow you to get an education,
    your lack of skills in the marketplace becomes an
    important consideration for the court. If you can prove
    to the court that you have few skills, they will deter-
    mine a greater need for rehabilitative alimony. This can
    include paying for you to get a college education.

4.  Medical reasons. If you can prove a valid long-term
    medical illness with a doctor's corroboration, a court
    will determine this as a basis for lifetime payments.
    When a man leaves his wife when she is ill, a court
    can be especially sympathetic to the wife.

5.  Psychological reasons. This allegation must be backed
    up by a psychologist or psychiatrist. It can be based
    upon abuse claims against your husband, or upon a
    simple claim of mental instability. Some of the more
    common theories presented to courts include:

    a.  Post-traumatic stress disorder, which has been
        exemplified by the long-term nightmares experi-
        enced by Vietnam war veterans. An acute event
        or series of events causing a traumatic shock to a
        person can create lifelong flashbacks of those
        events.

    b.  Major depression caused by abuse, requiring
        medication and counseling.

    c.  Development of a personality disorder brought
        on by your marriage and documented by your
        psychologist. Remember that if you choose this
        alternative, you most likely will be ordered to
        undergo an independent psychological evalua-
        tion by a psychologist chosen by your husband's
        lawyer. This other doctor may not agree with the
        diagnosis made by your own doctor. In most

cases, it is expected that the second opinion will contradict your doctor's opinion. When this type of expert fight occurs, the court will decide the matter using its own discretion.

6.  Length of marriage. In the past and in many states presently, the courts look at how long you and your husband have been married. When a wife has been married to her husband for a long time and the husband suddenly decides he no longer desires to remain with her, courts become sympathetic. The strength of your position in claiming long-term alimony can be augmented if you have been unemployed for a long period of time prior to the divorce suit.

These justifications for remaining unemployed are merely some of the ones that a court will find plausible. However, with some imagination you may be able to develop many other, equally acceptable reasons.

# Chapter 8 | *Establish Grounds for Child Custody*

Child custody and support are often the most critical and emotionally distressing aspects of a divorce situation. Unfortunately, children are often brought into their parents' divorce, and while this is difficult for the parents, it can be especially difficult for the children.

If children are an issue in your divorce, the situation should be dealt with sensitively and with great care, as bringing children into your divorce war is potentially very damaging to them. No matter what your other concerns are, the children should be the most important consideration in your divorce.

If you are successful in your struggle to retain custody of your children, you will receive child support from your ex-spouse. If, on the other hand, your husband is granted custody of the children, you will end up making the child support payments. Not only will you lose your children, you will be forced to relinquish all of your disposable income to your ex-spouse. Earning money to live is difficult enough. If the court orders you to pay child support, you will have an additional burden that may make your financial situation even more tenuous.

You should also keep in mind that child support payments are not considered taxable income, while alimony is. Because of this particular tax treatment, you want as much of your divorce settlement to be classified as monthly payment of child support.

In most states the court system will not make you prove where each and every dollar is spent. As long as you can show that your children are being well taken care of, you can spend or save the remaining money as you wish.

The more children you have, the more child support you should receive. Each state has a different method of calculating what you should receive for child support. Some states look at the income of both parents and use a chart to project the amount of child support the noncustodial parent should pay. In those states, your possible lack of income, or your lower income in relation to your husband's, provides a basis for you to request more. If your husband has a higher income, most states will require higher child support payments.

For the most part, child support payments are terminated at the child's eighteenth birthday. If your children are near this age of majority, the following advice does not apply to you. If you are an older mother with teenage children nearing adulthood, you should instead concentrate on receiving property settlement and alimony. Remember, child support payments will only provide a temporary reprieve and will not provide for your future or your children's. However, if you have younger children it will behoove you to maximize the child support you will receive by planning effectively.

At the outset, it is best to request a large payment and regularly ask for further increases. Many ex-wives will plan in advance to request an annual child support increase. If you can show the court that your husband has had a decrease in his cost of living or a raise in pay, you can request more child support. Keep in mind, however, that many ex-husbands will hide any evidence of new or higher income.

To discover this evidence, you can present your husband's tax returns to the court. Most courts will order tax returns to be provided to establish your husband's real income, but this will not necessarily indicate all of his additional income. For example, if he owns his own business, he may try to write off everything, including his boat, plane, or other luxury items. In such a situation, only a matrimonial lawyer and CPA will be able to scour the returns and other financial documents to find the hidden sources of income.

---

*Strategy 20.* *The level of child support payments will be determined by three factors: how many children you have, how high your husband's income is, and how low your own income is.*

---

# How the Courts Determine Custody

To receive child support, you have to be awarded physical custody of your children. Divorce lawyers representing husbands are aware of the importance of this factor. Consequently, your husband will know that he benefits if he has physical custody. The moment he consults with a divorce lawyer, he will be told how much money he will lose if he does not win custody. He will be told that the first spouse to file for divorce will obtain initial custody.

Women do not always get physical custody. If both parties are good parents, the court can award custody to either the wife or the husband. In some cases, split custody may be ordered, and no child support will be demanded of either party.

The old argument that the children are better off with their mothers is a relic of the past. Men are considered equally capable of parenting in the estimation of today's court system, and judges look at custodial issues objectively. In order to be awarded physical custody of your children, you need the testimony of experts to furnish the court with examples that distinguish you as the better parent.

In most states the courts look after the "best interests" of minor children. This judicial task involves many considerations, and several factors are reviewed that determine the court's final decision. A few of these factors are listed below.

1.  The age of the children. The younger the children, the greater the chance they will be awarded to the mother. Younger children are defined as five years of age or under.

2.  The gender of the children. An argument can be made that girls should stay with their mother and boys should stay with their father. This is not always the case. Many other factors can influence a judge's decision.

3.  The income of the parties. This factor can persuade a court to allow the children to reside with the parent who can best afford to take care of them.

4.  Evidence of child abuse by your husband. Child abuse claims against a husband are a weapon frequently used by wives. You must have more than an oral claim of abuse. Expert testimony from a psychologist or mental health worker will help establish these types of claims. Be wary—your husband can make the same type of claim against you.

5.  Relationship to other siblings. If the children have a tie to other half-brothers or half-sisters, it can be damaging to remove them from the home.

6.  The length of time the child has been under the actual care and control of any person other than you or your husband. Perhaps the children have been cared for by a grandparent or aunt. A court will weigh the fact that you have not personally been caring for the children against you or against your husband.

7.  The desires of the child regarding which parent they prefer to reside with. While this factor usually does not matter as much with children under the age of

fourteen, the court can still use the child's personal wishes as a factor.

8. The interaction and interrelationship of the child with each parent and with brothers and sisters. If one child does not get along with a brother or sister, the children may be split up and sent to live with different parents.

9. The child's attachment to his or her home, school, and community. A strong argument can be made for your children to remain where they are accustomed to living. Of course, you need to be awarded the house to make this argument work for you.

10. Evidence of spousal abuse against you. When a husband has abused his wife, an argument can be made that the husband has a problem with controlling his emotions or temper. Courts are concerned that such problems may lead to attacks on children.

11. Ties to grandparents. If one set of grandparents is alive and the other is not, the court will consider this when awarding custody. The children might be better off in an environment where they get attention from grandparents as well as the custodial parent.

This list illustrates how the court can look at a myriad of factors in attempting to determine child custody. Hundreds of other factors may come into play. Ultimately, you need to prove to the court that you are the parent who will best care for the children.

By obtaining a professional psychologist to explain in court that you should be awarded custody, you place yourself in a much better position. You can schedule a series of consultations with a psychologist who will observe the interaction between you and your children. If you show the psychologist your concern for your children, your strong bond with them, and your love for them, the psychologist is much more apt to testify in your favor.

Remember that even this evidence will not clinch the order of custody in your favor. You must evaluate all of the other factors—the psychologist is merely a building block in your overall case.

## Make a Link to a Forensic Psychologist

A forensic psychologist is one who is an authority on legal situations and is employed by parties specifically to testify in court. Your divorce lawyer should be able to suggest a good forensic psychologist, but the psychologist should meet at least a majority of the following requirements.

1. The psychologist is well recognized by the court and the judge who will decide your divorce.
2. The psychologist has a high level of credibility with the court in testifying both for women's and men's cases. Judges recognize a one-sided expert witness and give little credibility to those experts.
3. The psychologist has a substantial level of experience in dealing with child custody cases. You don't want the new kid on the block who is trying to build a reputation for himself.
4. The psychologist has more often than not been on the winning side of a custody battle. This means at least seventy-five percent of the parties for whom he or she testified won their custody battles.
5. The psychologist does not have a social or professional tie to your husband's lawyer that could result in the doctor showing his loyalty to the opposing side. This needs to be investigated. If your doctor receives more income from testifying for your husband's lawyer, he might become a turncoat witness.
6. The psychologist has strong ties to your divorce lawyer, which will tend to make him or her favor your position.

7.   The psychologist can help support your side from early consultations. Ask him questions. Do you believe I should get custody? Will you testify on my behalf to support having custody awarded to me rather than to my husband? Carefully evaluate his answers. If they are not positive, immediately stop having your children seen by that psychologist.

---

*Strategy 21. Be certain to hire a psychologist who is well recognized by your local divorce judges.*

---

If you take your children to a psychologist who does not support custody on your part, then even if you discontinue your visits, your husband will ultimately be able to call that psychologist to testify against you. In effect, you will have created a case against yourself.

Always check out the psychologist and evaluate how well he or she fits the criteria listed above, before you make any appointment. Once your children begin going to the psychologist, it is most likely too late. Your children will tell their father whom they went to. Once your husband knows that name, the psychologist can be called as a witness to support your husband's claim for custody.

## Convince Your Kids to Stay with You

Sadly, children often become strategic tools in a divorce situation, and bringing them into your personal battle should be avoided at all costs. However, if you believe that you are better equipped to take care of your children, you should do everything in your power to reassure them that they will be in a more secure and loving environment if they stay with you. It helps immeasurably to have your children request that the court allow them to live with you. On the other hand, if they express their wish to reside with your husband, it will definitely hurt your case.

Remember, if your children want to stay with their father and the court agrees, you will not receive child support—you will pay it. If you have an income, it can be significantly diminished by making child support payments. The courts care little for what the noncustodial spouse has to live on after the custody order. They are justifiably more concerned with putting the children in as positive an environment as possible in the postdivorce period.

## Establish Your Husband's Pattern of Bad Habits

If you genuinely believe that your husband is an unsuitable parent, or if he has displayed behavior that could impair his ability to properly raise your children, you must present these unfavorable qualities to the court. If you are able to prove to the court that your husband has any of the following traits, it is more likely that you will be able to convince the court that you are the parent best suited to take care of the children.

1.  Your husband is an alcoholic and drinks around the children, becoming abusive toward you and toward them.
2.  Your husband beats you, yells at you, or otherwise becomes abusive towards you.
3.  Your husband beats the children.
4.  Your husband uses drugs. Even if he only smokes marijuana, this is still a valid complaint against your husband that you can present to a court.
5.  Your husband has a gambling addiction. Squandering the family earnings can seriously jeopardize the family's financial status.

6.  Your husband never comes home early to stay with you and the children. He stays out with his friends drinking and carousing.
7.  Your husband has a mistress. He spends more time with her than with you and your children.
8.  Your husband is bisexual. He may have married you as a pretense to cover up his actual sexual preference.
9.  Your husband forces you to engage in unusual sex acts. A sex act can be considered unusual if you feel disgusted by the act and do not wish to engage in that type of sexual play.
10. Your husband is into pornography. This factor is much worse if it is child pornography.
11. Your husband has molested your children.
12. Your husband works long hours, and does not spend time with the family.
13. Your husband permits your children to become involved in criminal activities (e.g., smoking marijuana, shoplifting, destroying property).

There are dozens of traits that can characterize your husband as an unfit father in the court's assessment. The more of these unfavorable traits your husband displays, the lesser his chances of being awarded custody. Make a list of all of these traits and present it to your attorney, who will determine which may be significant to the particular judge who presides over your divorce.

You can also prove many of these unfavorable traits by talking to your psychologist about them. The following case history illustrates how this can affect the outcome of a custody battle.

Mary had been married for nine years and was thirty-two years old when she filed for divorce. Throughout her marriage, her husband had caused her a tremendous amount of aggravation.

Mary and her husband had two children—one boy, age eight, and one girl, age six. Although the children were still young, they were old enough that the court would at least consider their desires in awarding custody. Both parents worked full-time, and the children routinely stayed with baby sitters when not in school. In other words, Mary could not show the court that she stayed at home and took care of the children more often than her husband.

The boy wanted to stay with the father. The little girl wanted to stay with Mary. In this case, the custody decision could go either way. Mary listened to advice of counsel and attended sessions with a psychologist who was favorable to her position in the case. This particular psychologist regularly testified for both sides in divorce cases. In counseling, Mary complained that her husband was often drunk at night and stayed out late. She also reported that on occasion, the children had answered the phone when their father's mistress called asking for their daddy. While Mary's husband did not beat her or the children, he did scream and yell in front of them, causing them to cry and become withdrawn.

The psychologist prepared a report indicating these traits, in which she noted the angry tendencies of the father and recommended the children reside with the mother so that they would not become further withdrawn. Psychological testing backed up the opinion of the doctor. At trial, Mary won custody of her children along with a large child support award until the children's eighteenth birthdays.

Without the testimony of the psychologist, the court would have had no basis for its decision, other than the testimony of Mary and her husband—and most likely each of them would have claimed the other was a bad parent.

In this case, it was the expert testimony that provided the extra evidence Mary needed to win custody.

In this case, the mother was able to support her claims with the help of expert testimony. Keep in mind, however, that although this approach may help you in your custody battle, it may affect your children negatively. Ultimately, it is up to you to decide what is best for your children. You should involve them in your divorce only if it is absolutely necessary for their long-term happiness.

# Chapter 9 | *Ways to Convince Your Husband to Divorce You*

If your relationship has lapsed into a state of marital doldrums and you are consistently bored by your husband, you should begin to evaluate your situation. Does your husband treat you disrespectfully or offensively? Has he been unfaithful to you? Does he stay out late drinking with his buddies? After years of loving devotion and support, have you simply had enough of his inconsiderate behavior?

Most likely, if you answer yes to any of these questions, you did not develop your convictions overnight. You probably have reminded him continually to be more conscious of your feelings. Yet despite your efforts, he has continued behaving in a way that is not only hurtful to you, but altogether unacceptable.

If your husband insists that he loves you and you discover, for example, that he is choosing to spend his time fishing or playing golf rather than spending it with you, chances are he is simply taking advantage of the situation. Remember, a man would rather not disrupt a relationship which allows him to get away with whatever he wants. If your husband is adulterous, disrespectful, or generally inconsiderate and you allow this behavior to continue without consequence, he will not change his ways. Usually, it is up to the woman to bring an end to such a relationship.

You should realize, first of all, that many women feel a similar sense of rejection or emptiness, and secondly, that you can create an opportunity to remedy the situation. By convincing him to divorce you, you will enable yourself to gain the freedom you need to take control of your life and start anew.

## Criticize Him Daily

Your husband will begin to dislike you more and more if you learn to criticize everything he does. Don't leave anything to the imagination. Pick out his best quality and consistently tear it down, or find his weakest point and continually remind him of it—use these tactics to intimidate him. After a short period of time, he will believe you hate him even if you don't. By carving into his ego like a Thanksgiving turkey, you can effectively break down his self-esteem.

Your husband may have certain attributes that disturb him more than others. For example, if he is concerned that he is balding, make certain that you notice his thinning hair, receding hairline, or bald spot. Or perhaps you husband has a pudgy stomach or love handles and his clothes no longer fit. Maybe he has acne or a weak voice. You can point out all of these characteristics in front of his friends and family and embarrass him.

Typically, the easiest way to deflate a man's ego is by criticizing his lovemaking techniques. A man's self-image is greatly affected by his perception of his virility. If you degrade his sexual ability, you will essentially emasculate him—his entire sense of self-worth will be dismantled.

Compare your husband to other men and subtly indicate that you find them more attractive. Point out the fitness buff at the gym, the movie star, or even the man next door. Or tell your husband that he dresses poorly, and whenever possible, attempt to outdo him by wearing a stunning outfit to a casual event.

Most importantly, make sure that you always question him about every spare moment of time he spends away from you. Do this, not perfunctorily, but in an accusing and deliberate manner. Remind him of all of the unfair things he has done to you, even if it has been years since he committed them. Accuse him of drinking, using drugs, sleeping with other women, sleeping with other men, and anything else that might place him on the defensive. He will spend his hours away from you worrying how to explain his absence, regardless of how exemplary his conduct has been.

Finally, mention your ex-lover, ex-husband, or ex-boyfriend just to spite him. Tell him how much better all of them were in bed or how completely devoted they were, and point out their physical or intellectual superiority.

There are many ways to criticize your husband. You simply need to observe his weaknesses and prey on his insecurities.

## Accuse Him of Having Affairs

Nothing will aggravate your husband more than accusing him of an affair that he has not had. If you accuse him repeatedly, it is highly likely that he will begin to have an affair just to spite you for the continued accusations. In other words, if he must bear the harassment, he will probably feel that he might as well have an actual affair.

Ultimately, he is either going to leave you to escape the accusations, or start having an affair. Once he has this affair, you can use it to sue him for the emotional distress he has caused you with a marital tort claim. Either way, you achieve your goal.

There probably are numerous candidates for your accusations. You can accuse him of having an affair with his secretary, or perhaps the next-door neighbor whose husband is a traveling salesman. Of course, there is always your best friend, who may even be able to assist you with your scheme. However, be careful not to tell her too much—if she begins to sympathize with your husband, your plan can go awry. In a worst-case scenario, she will end up with the financial assets you rightfully deserve.

Your goal in this instance is not to rid yourself of your good friends, but to rid yourself of the husband who has abused you. Your husband may be able to use his wealth as a powerful tool to turn your friends against you. Be wary of those friends who hang on for financial gain in contrast to true friends who love and cherish you. The grass is always greener on the other side of the fence. Be certain you know your friend, her loyalty to you, and your certainty in her absolute devotion to you as a friend before revealing any information to her.

Imprint lipstick on his white collar and apply perfume to the shirt. Allow the shirt to sit for a week or two and then bring it to his attention some evening when he is in a romantic mood. Accusing him of having an adulterous affair will abruptly change his mood and exacerbate his resentment.

Over time, you will be able to wear him down to his point of least resistance. Either he will tire of the continued accusations and request a divorce, or he will gladly grant one upon your terms.

*Strategy 22.* *When you want a divorce, learn to aggravate your husband whenever possible, but never engage in conduct that might be construed as detrimental to your position in the divorce.*

# Lend His Money to Your Relatives

Financial matters often cause arguments between spouses, and lending money to relatives is an especially good catalyst for a fight. Ask your husband to lend money to your brother, father, sister, aunt, or any other relative you have, no matter how remote. If he refuses to lend money to them, fight with him over his reluctance to part with funds from his stockpile of wealth. Refuse to sleep with him because of his greed.

Furthermore, tell your relatives to call your husband at his office. Make sure that they do this independently of your loan requests. Have your relatives ask for substantial amounts for critical debts such as car or mortgage payments. If your husband refuses their supposedly earnest requests, accuse him of being miserly and coldhearted.

The following case history will provide you with a scenario in which a wife's request for loans eventually led to a divorce settlement in her favor.

> When Belinda married a wealthy attorney, she professed her love for him and expressed her wish that they have a long and wonderful life together. However, unbeknownst to her husband, Belinda was simply entering into the marriage with the hope of eventually receiving some of his wealth.
>
> During the last few months of their marriage, she began to request that her husband lend money to her brother to pay rent on his home in Florida, which was $2,400 a month. The husband knew that if the brother could not pay his rent, he certainly would not be able to pay back the loan. Belinda then began to complain regularly to her husband that her father was losing the battle in his business and needed financial help.
>
> Belinda's husband was shrewd enough to realize that Belinda was actually trying to obtain funds to pay for her own divorce. He refused to lend any money to her relatives. Belinda became increasingly angry over this refusal and intensified her efforts. Within a few short months, her husband could no longer stand the constant requests for financial aid to her relatives. He filed for divorce. Even though *he* filed, Belinda convinced the divorce judge that her husband was a

greedy miser who would not help her ailing mother. The judge was sympathetic to her situation and awarded her more in the settlement.

Your goal is three-pronged: first, to convince your husband to divorce you or grant you a divorce; second, to obtain money for your divorce or simply spend the loans given to your relatives; and third, to hide money in this manner so that the divorce court will not charge it against you when you file for a divorce. After all, it was not you who borrowed the money, it was your relatives.

## Run up His Credit Cards

There is a dependable way to put aside money and assets which will most likely be awarded to you in the divorce. Normally, the divorce court will award a party all the personal property, belongings, and effects in his or her possession at the time of the divorce filing. Courts do not like to make rulings on every small item of personal property that a party may own, as the goal of the court is to quickly end the litigation between the parties.

Only rarely will the court take away a wife's jewelry, clothing, shoes, handbags, furs, or other personal belongings. The rationale is quite simple. Over the years, domestic judges tire of the mundane nature of divorce cases and are reluctant to get involved in such petty details of property division. Each spouse always accuses the other of wrongdoing and lies in court about the facts in order to win. Each spouse holds firmly to his or her convictions, regardless of their validity. Each case presents a new couple arguing in the same manner over the same issues. Most judges do not like to hear divorce cases and normally attempt to shift them to other judges with more patience. Usually, one or two tireless judges will agree to accept the docket of divorce cases.

With this in mind, use your husband's credit cards to buy personal property for yourself. Request that he place your name on all of his credit cards so that you can use them freely. Go to new merchants and obtain credit cards in his name without his knowledge, using his credit as a guarantee of your ability to pay.

Obtain as many credit cards as possible, and when the bills come to your home, pay the minimum due without showing the bills to your husband. You can spend a fortune over two or three months and pay only the minimum fee. As long as the purchases are personal items such as handbags, expensive ladies' jewelry, clothing, furs, and other similar purchases, the court will allow you to keep the property in the divorce.

If you are unemployed and your husband makes sufficient income, most likely he will either agree to pay the credit card bills or be ordered by the court to pay them. However, be careful to spread the purchases out over an extended period of time so the court will assume your husband approved all of the purchases. If you go on a spending spree just prior to filing for divorce, the court may recognize your plan and order you to pay the bills.

---

*Strategy 23.* *Get all credit cards in your husband's name to limit your liability for the debt after the divorce. You should be careful to understand that cash advances should be used to aid the marital estate and not to rob the estate of assets. You are never advised to perjure yourself before the court by stating an alternative purpose other than what is true.*

---

Sara was married to a wealthy man who scrupulously counted every cent he acquired. When the love between them had ended, Sara obtained legal advice on how to shelter some of the property purchases made with her husband's assets. Over several months, a plan was developed. Sara charged every gold or platinum card to its highest limit, but as the bills came in, she paid only the minimum due. She was able to pay the minimum fees from the meager allowance furnished by her husband. She made applications for numerous cards from all the major credit card companies and from all of the retail merchants in her city. Over eight or nine months, she was able to purchase over sixty thousand dollars of personal property that the court would award to her in the settlement. She bought new designer clothes, expensive handbags, tennis bracelets, necklaces, and rings. In addition, she stashed away almost ten thousand dollars in cash, which was rendered untraceable.

The last issue resolved at the divorce table between Sara and her husband was, not surprisingly, the responsibility for repayment of the credit cards. Her husband earned more than $250,000 a year, and so, rather than risk the judge's unknown verdict, he settled and assumed responsibility for the tens of thousands of dollars of credit card debt that Sara had built up over several months.

In this case history, the wife thoroughly planned her strategy. You, too, need to be careful in the implementation of your plan. If your husband finds out that you obtained numerous credit cards and charged heavily on them, he can cancel the cards as easily as you obtained them. He must not become aware of this plan until after you have filed for divorce. Remember, if necessary, you can obtain cash advances on the credit cards to make the minimum payments required each month.

## Nag, Nag, Nag

You know your husband—his mind, his abilities, and his weaknesses—better than any other person. You can use this knowledge to your benefit by manipulating your husband's ego. Remember, his self-esteem is shaped by your opinions of him. If you flatter and praise him, his ego will be hugely inflated. If, on the other hand, you criticize and degrade him, he will lose all of his confidence. If you alternate between these emotional states, your husband will not know if you love or hate him, and this confusion will enable you to take advantage of the situation.

When your husband feels insecure about your relationship, he will probably try to win back your favor by buying you gifts. However, keep in mind that your plan has a dual goal. First, you are attempting to persuade him to buy you gifts by convincing him that you love him, and second, you are trying to push him into giving you a divorce. It takes diligence and effort to vacillate between these opposing goals, and depending on your husband's emotional strength, he may respond differently. You will need to carefully monitor his feelings in order to maximize your gains. Remember, if you can persuade your husband to buy you expensive gifts, you will be able to keep them in the divorce settlement.

*Strategy 24.* *Control your husband by being alternately loving and indifferent to keep him in a state of continual concern.*

By consciously building your husband up and tearing him down, you will not only weaken him over time, but will be able to make substantial acquisitions during the same period. If you make a list citing all of his good qualities in one column and all of his lesser qualities in another, it should provide you with additional justification for your behavior.

# Part Two | *Are You Ready for Battle?*

# Chapter 10 | *How to Prove Marital Torts Against Your Husband*

In recent years, a new area of law has developed which will enable you to sue your husband and obtain more from the divorce settlement than was previously possible. With a marital tort, which is a legal claim that you can make against your husband for any personal injuries he caused you, you have the ability to bring a civil lawsuit against your husband regardless of your marital circumstances. In most marriages, a certain degree of emotional or mental stress will arise from everyday occurrences or interactions. With a marital tort claim, this type of ordinary stress is sufficient basis for a lawsuit.

In order to better understand this type of lawsuit, it will help to review how the law has treated women. In England, where our present laws evolved, women were not allowed to own property in their own name or enter into contracts. A woman could not be sued by another person without joining her husband in the lawsuit. Women had virtually no rights and no legal identities apart from their husbands'.

Similarly, women's rights in the United States evolved slowly. For hundreds of years, women were considered chattel, or property owned by men. In other words, a husband owned his wife as personal property. It seems incomprehensible that this archaic principle of law existed in this country, but it did.

Over time, however, the laws in the U.S. changed. Beginning in the nineteenth century, laws known as Married Women's Acts were created that gave married women legal rights, and the classification of a wife as chattel became extinct.

The passage of the Nineteenth Amendment in 1920, which gave women the constitutional right to vote, marked an immediate and significant change in the status of women. Ultimately, this amendment not only gave women voting rights but began to provide equality to women.

Furthermore, another doctrine of law developed, called interspousal immunity, that prohibited a spouse from bringing a lawsuit against the other spouse. This doctrine was supposedly necessary because of our court system's public policy, which was formulated to maintain family harmony and unity. Essentially, however, this meant that a husband could physically abuse his wife without any potential legal consequence. In effect, men created a system to protect themselves from women.

However, as women have gained more legal equality, and with their increasing presence in the legal and judicial systems, the doctrine of interspousal immunity has slowly but steadily eroded.

At last count, a majority of states have abolished the doctrine of interspousal immunity. With this abolishment, new forms of lawsuits have emerged that allow wives to bring complaints under a variety of legal theories that never before could have been brought to court.

Appendix A at the end of this book lists the states that have abrogated or abolished the doctrine of interspousal immunity. Some states have only partially abolished this ancient law. Some states have abolished the doctrine only in the case of a motor vehicle accident. Allowing spouses to sue one another for a motor vehicle accident gives the couple access to car insurance that otherwise would be unattainable.

Several states allow couples to sue each other in tort only after the marriage has been ended or after they have been separated. Other states have totally abolished the doctrine, allowing married couples to sue one another in all instances.

The law is changing rapidly, so it is impossible for this book to give the exact status of law in any given state. Only an attorney in your area will be able to properly inform you of the current status of the law allowing you to sue your spouse in tort. You may not be able to bring a marital tort suit against your husband in every instance.

Traditionally, all you can seek in a divorce is property distribution, alimony, and child support. By adding a marital tort suit, you are allowed to sue your husband under a myriad of legal theories to get additional compensation that you would normally not receive. A marital tort suit is much like playing the horses at the track and winning a trifecta. Usually, your individual winnings come from each race, but when you win a trifecta, your winnings rise exponentially. By rolling the dice with a marital tort suit, you can let the court decide just how despicable your husband is, and how much compensation you should get for putting up with him for so many years.

Filing a tort case against a husband can create leverage to get a larger divorce settlement. If you file the additional lawsuit, you can ask for more in the divorce and agree to drop the marital tort suit. Your husband will be scared enough of the divorce case; when you file a second suit alleging that he harmed you physically or emotionally and you are debilitated as a result of this abuse, he will spend every waking moment in fear of the potential consequences. His attention will be turned away from business to the legal nightmare at hand—he won't believe the nightmare is real until he pays and pays.

An advantage of these particular legal suits is that you don't have to have solid proof as a basis for a claim to sue. Circumstantial evidence, like the evidence in many murder trials where the killer is not seen pulling the trigger, can be used effectively. The entire claim can be structured on your oral statements of evidence concerning his actions toward you.

However, it is highly beneficial to have corroborating evidence to bolster and support your allegations. Many courts seem to find assertions of mental stress, corroborated by the testimony of a psychological expert, to be substantial cause to sue. In most cases, the court will not dismiss the claim even if there are no witnesses. It is similar to a rape case in which there are only two parties to tell what happened. In such cases, one person must win, and the other, by necessity, must lose. The same is true in a marital tort claim—only one of you will win. The most convincing witness is the winner.

Another potential benefit of a marital tort claim is that a lawyer will pursue the claim on a contingency fee basis, for a percentage of the damages awarded by the court. Suppose you are awarded one hundred thousand dollars by the court. Your lawyer might take one-third or more of the judgment as his fee, depending upon the amount you agreed to in the contract. This means that if the lawyer does not win the case, you don't have to pay the attorney fees. However, be careful to get the lawyer to agree to pay all the expenses of the suit in the event of a loss, or you could end up paying them.

Lawyers who are experienced and knowledgeable are able to assess the value of your claim at the beginning of the case. When a lawyer is afraid to front the expenses out of his own pocket it can mean one of only a few things: first, that he is uncertain whether you have a case; second, that he cannot determine the exact value of your case, and he is unwilling to risk his own money; third, that he is too inexperienced to evaluate the case value. When a lawyer has experience and knows the value of a case he will roll the dice and spend his own money to finance your case, betting on the final outcome. Beware the lawyer who is afraid to express an opinion and front the expenses. In the end, you may be the one paying money out of your pocket. Not to your husband, but even worse yet—to your lawyer.

## How to Prove Marital Torts Against Your Husband

Basically, by filing a marital tort claim, you can't lose. At worst, you will get free representation on a percentage that will enable you to harass your husband for a year or more in court. At best, you will win an award for thousands and perhaps millions of dollars, in addition to getting your divorce award.

Remember, it does not matter how long you have been married. You can bring a marital tort action against your husband even if you have been married for only a few short months. If your husband treated you so badly in that short period of time and you have suffered permanent damage as a result, you deserve compensation.

> Vicki married her husband after knowing him for only a short time. She soon learned that he had a volatile temper. His rages were volcanic. The worse he treated her, the more withdrawn she became. He began to have an extramarital affair a few months after the marriage began. Both knew the marriage was a horrible mistake and a miserable learning experience. Vicki's husband began to verbally torment her to the point of making her cry uncontrollably.
>
> Vicki went to her lawyer for legal advice. He told her that she needed to document every act of abuse. She started counseling with a psychologist for the depression she was suffering from her husband's outrageous bursts of anger. Her lawyer advised her to call the police if things got out of hand.
>
> One night when Vicki and her husband were both drinking, he began screaming at her with rage she had not seen before. When he threw a vase at her and then broke a chair against the wall, barely missing her head, she called the police to have them stop the argument.
>
> The broken vase and chair proved to the police that a bad fight had occurred. Her husband was charged with assault in a marital situation.
>
> Since Vicki's marriage was short-lived her lawyer told her she would get almost nothing from the divorce. In addition to the divorce action, she filed a marital tort action alleging marital abuse. It stated that she suffered from mental anguish and would need continued counseling.
>
> Shortly thereafter, the two cases were settled and her violent husband agreed to pay her seventy-five thousand dollars to settle both claims.

The following sections discuss the most commonly filed marital tort claims.

# Intentional Infliction of Emotional Distress

If revenge and the desire to destroy your husband are the prevailing motivators in your divorce, this is the type of lawsuit which will best help you reach your goals. These are the easiest claims to make, and the boundaries are limited only by your ingenuity. You simply need to convincingly claim that your husband intentionally or recklessly caused you severe emotional distress. Your husband, on the other hand, has the more difficult task of disproving your claim.

Since most courts want to believe that people do not tell lies under oath, your assertions will be more readily believable. Of course, this does not mean that you should lie in court—perjury is punishable by fines and prison sentences—but you can effectively prove that you have undergone mental duress from the breakup of the marriage. Every marriage that comes to an end provides sufficient stress for this claim. But remember, the more evidence you have to prove your claims, the more realistic chance you will have of winning in court.

If your husband did behave in an emotionally abusive way toward you, you have an additional basis for this type of claim. If he yelled at you, insulted you, or came home drunk, these occurrences can be considered emotional abuse. With all of these situations, you will need the corroboration of a psychologist. Once you have enlisted the help of an expert to testify on your behalf, you can openly make these claims without any fear of being charged with perjury.

Proof is important to your case. Document every conceivable action on the part of your husband that causes you suffering.

Keep in mind that psychological testimony is subject to a high degree of interpretation—ten different experts may have ten different opinions. Ultimately, no one knows how accurate a psychological interpretation is because of the subjective nature of any given person's emotional distress. This means that your assertions can never be proven or disproven beyond a shadow of a doubt.

Remember, anything that emotionally bothers you can become a basis for a lawsuit. Did your husband suggest you have a facelift or breast implants, or require you to undergo any other cosmetic surgery? Or did he look at other women, making you feel inferior? Did he visit strip clubs with his friends? Did he force you to wear certain clothes that you didn't like?

All of these actions can be used to prove that your husband was either intentionally manipulating you or attempting to shatter your self-esteem, or both. You will certainly be able to find a psychologist who will agree that your husband has damaged you emotionally for life.

Remember, your husband has not behaved perfectly throughout the marriage—this is your chance to get back at him for all the wrong he has done you.

---

*Strategy 25.* *Every divorce case has a silver lining. The mental stress caused by your husband provides a basis to sue for a marital tort.*

---

The following case history illustrates that although a woman may suffer immeasurably during her marriage, she does have an avenue of revenge.

Angela had been married to her third husband for six years. During these six years, her husband had affairs with younger women, convinced Angela to have plastic surgery to make her appear more youthful, changed the way she dressed, and routinely degraded her.

Without a marital tort claim, the marriage would have allowed her to receive only several years of alimony and half of the equity from the couple's home. Angela, however, started to see a psychologist eight months prior to filing for divorce and divulged everything to him. The psychologist discovered that Angela had a history of emotional problems and had suffered from low self-esteem, bouts of depression, paranoia, and various other psychological disorders. The psychologist was willing to testify against her current husband to help restore Angela's self-esteem and confidence. He was able to state an opinion that her husband's actions had revived and aggravated her pre-existing conditions, which had become dormant with time.

Immediately after the divorce was filed, Angela requested a hefty sum of cash from her husband and threatened to ruin his life if he did not pay her the money. When the husband refused to comply with this request, Angela followed through with a marital tort case, claiming every act of bad faith her husband had committed. With these claims and the psychologist's help, she was able to win the case.

Ultimately, the marital tort suit cost her husband more than one hundred thousand dollars to defend. When he lost the suit, he had to pay Angela several hundred thousand dollars to terminate the suit.

The divorce case never went to trial. Just before trial, her husband's attorney advised him the payment of several hundred thousand dollars was a better option than risking a million-dollar judgment. In addition, Angela was provided with two years of alimony to get her back on her feet, as well as her share of the house. In this case, had it not been for this additional lawsuit, Angela would have received little or nothing.

This case history shows that even in a marriage where the husband was not wholly responsible for the mental and emotional distress, the wife still won. In the legal sense, it does not matter if you are 100 percent right or wrong, as long as you have a psychologist to testify on your behalf and a lawyer to pursue your claim.

Even if you have signed a prenuptial or postnuptial marriage contract that limits your rights in a divorce, you can still pursue a marital tort under this theory. Those contracts, in most instances, will not save your husband if these types of suits are filed. By making soap opera-esque allegations against your husband, you will be the victor—the spoils go to you.

*Strategy 26. A marital tort suit may allow you to receive more than your marriage contract agrees to.*

# Domestic Violence

Domestic violence claims provide four ways for you to go after your husband:

1.  You can file a divorce action, claiming incompatibility and fault based upon his verbal and physical abuse.
2.  You can file a marital tort claim with the divorce action.
3.  You can file a criminal action against your husband and seek his incarceration.
4.  You can file a civil rights violations claim under the Violence Against Women Act of 1994.

You can prove that your husband verbally assaulted or physically battered you with or without photographic evidence. When a fight erupts between you and your husband, call 911, report the fight, and request police intervention. When the police arrive, tell them your husband screamed at you, hit you, or otherwise attacked you. Fully list all of his actions so that a complete police report is created to prove your case.

Wait for an opportunity when your husband has alcohol on his breath. His intoxication will substantially increase the credibility of your claim. Police are well trained at detecting intoxication, with or without a breath test. Furthermore, because of the physical size differences between men and women and preconceived societal notions, the judicial system will almost always believe a woman in matters of domestic violence. The police report will substantiate your abuse claims in court.

However, be careful that you don't go overboard in your allegations. You might end up getting your husband placed in jail, which will prevent him from earning income to pay your alimony or monetary damages won in a law suit. An uncollectable judgment for millions has no value.

Like an emotional distress claim, an assault and battery claim can be proven without physical evidence. That is to say, your genuine assertion that an instance of domestic violence took place will usually be enough evidence in the court's estimation. Your credibility on the claim is to be determined by the judge or jury. Remember, society and the judicial system want to rectify centuries of abuse inflicted against women. In other words, they want to believe you.

> Beth needed to prove claims against her husband that she had never documented with physical evidence such as photographs or police reports. Her husband had abused her, and she believed she was entitled to bring a marital tort claim.
>
> At the urging of her lawyer, she invited a close friend to come to her house on a night when she knew her husband would be out drinking. The friend hid her car down the street. When they heard the husband's car pulling into the garage, Beth's friend quickly moved downstairs where she would not be seen. Sure enough, a few minutes later, an argument erupted. Her husband had no idea his rude and violent outbursts were being overheard and would be used in a later court action.
>
> At the preliminary court hearing, Beth's friend provided credible corroboration of her claims of abuse. Her friend stood up well to intense scrutiny under cross-examination. Once the judge heard this additional evidence, Beth's husband's lawyer advised her husband to increase his settlement offer before the judge's ruling.

# Sexual Torts

If your husband has given you some form of sexually transmitted disease, you can file a sexual tort claim. This may seem unfathomable, but not only does this happen, in the last three decades these kinds of lawsuits have appeared with greater frequency. Often, they are cases in which the husband is alleged to have had extramarital affairs.

If you bring a lawsuit against your husband for a sexual tort, generally you must prove that you did not know he had the disease. For example, if he had herpes for years before the marriage and informed you of this, then your knowledge of his condition may ruin your case. In order to win this particular claim, you will have to prove that he concealed his disease from you. Had you known that your husband became infected from sexual relations with his mistress, chances are you would not have slept with him. But if you chose to marry him with knowledge of the disease, then you have no real legal reason to complain.

This follows the old doctrine of law called assumption of the risk. When you decide to go bungee jumping, you assume the risk of death. When you have sex with a person carrying a known disease, you assume a risk that you may contract the disease.

Many home insurance policies with liability coverage will cover this claim. However, the policy may have contractual clauses that provide the insurance company with a defense enabling it to refuse payment.

Juries are appalled when they hear that a husband has inflicted a sexually transmitted disease on his trusting wife, and while this may help you win the case, it is not necessarily a weapon that you want the ability to use. Frankly, the monetary award is not enough compensation for the disease.

# Abuse

In today's society, any misconduct on your husband's part that disturbs the harmony of your marital relationship can be considered abusive. This abuse can be physical or verbal. If your husband battered, tormented, or assaulted you, these are all examples of abuse. If he told you that you are fat, ignorant, or from a low-class family, these statements are also abusive.

Perhaps your husband yells at you as if you were a dog. Maybe he swears at you when your mother calls or comes by for a visit. Keep in mind that abuse does not have to be monumental—anything from major battery to the smallest insult can become a basis for an abuse claim. The more of these claims you can bring to a court, the greater your chances for presenting the court with an abusive behavior pattern.

As long as your psychologist is willing to substantiate your claims, you will have sufficient proof of abuse. You should also keep a diary in which you write every negative action your husband makes on a daily basis. When it comes time to sue, you can use your diary as proof of your husband's behavior. Be careful to maintain your diary regularly, as any gaps in your narrative can lead a jury to believe that these omissions indicate periods of stable, or even happy, relations. Make sure you are consistent and conscientious—no matter how trivial the conduct might seem, it can still provide a basis for a marital tort claim.

You have the ability to reveal to a court just how miserably your husband treated you. A jury will be permitted to hear exactly how your husband swore at you, ignored you, or made you feel worthless and unloved. If you are fortunate enough to get the right jury, you will have an opportunity to be more than adequately compensated for your suffering. You can tip the scales of justice in your favor. Your husband took part of your life from you, and now you can utilize your ingenuity and skills to get it back.

# Negligence

A negligent act is one that arises out of carelessness or thoughtlessness, and is not brought about intentionally. For example, a careless driver who overlooks a red light and hits another car commits a negligent act. Similarly, if your husband is intoxicated and hurts you unintentionally, he commits a negligent act, thereby presenting you with an opportunity to make a marital tort claim based on negligent behavior.

The advantage of claiming negligence in a marital tort is that a homeowners' insurance policy can cover the bill. If your husband is not particularly wealthy, this may be an excellent avenue to pursue. However, there are some limitations on this type of claim.

First of all, you need to find a lawyer who thoroughly understands personal injury suits and can interpret insurance policies to determine if any given policy can provide coverage for such a claim. If he or she is successful in getting the insurance company to foot the bill, you could receive a large sum for your claim.

Keep in mind, however, that lawyers will only take on cases that will ultimately earn them fees. If your husband is not wealthy, the lawyer may not be willing to fight the case without a big potential payoff, and will be less likely to argue the claim on a contingency fee for a percentage. If he feels your claim is not substantial enough, he may not take your case, leaving you with no alternative but to sue for another type of marital tort.

Secondly, insurance companies have recently begun to exclude all types of marital tort claims from homeowners' insurance policies. Women's organizations are going to have to lobby diligently to ensure that federal legislation is introduced that will prevent insurance companies from excluding marital tort claims by arguing on the basis of equal legal protection.

Nevertheless, because marital torts are a recent development, not all insurance policies entirely exclude coverage for them. A lawyer with expertise in this area will be able to establish which type of exclusions your policy may have, or better yet, will cleverly circumvent these exclusions altogether.

## Fraudulent Inducement to Marry

Marriage induced by fraud is rare, but it does occur. When it occurs, it is a sad event. This claim is based upon your proving that your husband somehow convinced or induced you to marry him on a fraudulent basis.

The most frequent basis for this claim is when a husband commits bigamy, marrying you when he was not yet divorced from his other wife. Some cases have claimed that a new husband promised to pay to his wife the alimony that she had been receiving from her previous husband if the new marriage ended before the expiration of the original alimony term from the old husband. Another case was brought by a wife who claimed she was supporting her husband through medical school. He began having an affair during the marriage and fraudulently concealed this fact from her so that she would continue to work to put him through medical school. A Virginia appeals court allowed her to pursue this claim based upon fraud.

To prove a claim of this type, you have to establish the following legal events or factors:

1. Your husband made a false representation to you.
2. He had knowledge that his representation to you was false.
3. He intended to induce you to rely on his misrepresentation.
4. You justifiably relied upon his representation, which was false.
5. Because of your reliance on his false representation, you were injured or damaged.

Claims of this nature are much harder to establish. A skilled lawyer will be able to help determine if you have a claim of this type.

# Civil Rights for Women

When President Clinton signed his new crime bill into law in September of 1994, he not only made a step forward in the fight against crime, but also established a new civil right for women. Until this bill became law, gender-motivated violence against women was not considered a violation of civil rights. This new law has created one more protective measure for women.

Gender motivation means that an act of violence was committed against a woman because she is female. For example, you must prove in court that your husband verbally abused women or made derogatory comments about women to show his ill will toward women in general. In simple terms, if he abused you and you can prove that it was because of a general misogynistic attitude, then you may have a civil rights action.

The new law is called the Civil Rights Remedies for Gender-Motivated Violence or the Violence Against Women Act of 1994. These are some of the more important provisions of this important new law.

(a) **Purpose.** Under the affirmative powers of Congress, the purpose of this subtitle is to protect civil rights victims of gender-motivated violence, and to promote public safety, health, and activities affecting interstate commerce by establishing a Federal civil rights cause of action for victims of crimes of violence motivated by gender.

(b) **Right to Be Free From Crimes of Violence.** All persons within the United States shall have the right to be free from crimes of violence motivated by gender (as defined in subsection (d)).

(c)　**Cause of Action.** A person who commits a crime of violence and thus deprives another of the right in subsection (b) shall be accountable for the crime he committed, and will be subject to compensatory and punitive damages, as well as any other punishment as a court deems appropriate.

(d)　**Definitions.** For the purposes of this section—

(1)　the term "crime of violence motivated by gender" means a crime of violence committed because of gender, or on the basis of gender, and due, at least in part, to a dislike of a victim's gender, and

(2)　the term "crimes of violence" means—

(A)　an act or series of acts that would constitute a felony against a person, or a felony against property if it poses a risk of physical injury to another person.

(B)　an act or series of acts that would constitute a felony described in subparagraph (A).

One of the most important aspects of this new law is that there is no requirement that your husband actually be charged with a crime. His actions against you need only be ones which would be considered felonies if he were to be prosecuted. Eliminating the prosecution and conviction elements from these acts means that you can bring a civil rights violation suit against your husband claiming that the act or acts would have been felonies if you had filed a criminal complaint.

Conceivably, this law would apply to a domestic battery case in which your husband has acted criminally with the intent to harm you. However, your husband's criminal act must rise to the level of a felony in your state in order for you to have a valid civil rights claim. Most incidents of domestic battery are not more than misdemeanors, so they are not considered civil rights violations. On the other hand, if your husband attacked you and caused serious bodily injury it may be considered aggravated battery—a felony and a violation of your civil rights, regardless of whether your husband was criminally charged.

## How to Prove Marital Torts Against Your Husband

Many different types of acts against you or your personal property might qualify as violations of your civil rights. A few, but certainly not all, of these are listed below:

1.  Aggravated battery. This is more than merely being hit. If you are severely beaten, requiring hospitalization, or if a weapon is used against you, the actions may qualify to be considered aggravated battery.
2.  Marital rape, if a crime in your state.
3.  Destruction of your property, serious enough to be a felony. Take the example where your husband rams his car into your car or garage. Another example might be where he has attempted to destroy your house by arson.
4.  Intentionally transmitting certain types of sexually transmitted diseases in states where the knowing transmission of disease to another person is a felony. This could be AIDS, herpes, gonorrhea, syphilis, or many other sexually transmitted diseases.
5.  Repeated violence against a woman when the man has been convicted of battery before. Some states make a series of convictions a felony. The "three times and you're out" law allows some states to consider a person more dangerous if he has committed a sufficient number of prior violent crimes.

Certainly there are other acts committed by men that will qualify as violations of civil rights. If you have been the unfortunate victim of such a civil rights violation, you will have some advantages when it comes time to fight your divorce in court. With a normal marital tort claim, the responsibility for paying the attorney fees is yours, but in a civil rights suit, you can bring a claim for attorney fees in addition to your claim for compensation.

Furthermore, in a civil rights suit, you have greater leverage because of recent government legislation. That is to say, by making a civil rights claim rather than an ordinary marital tort claim, you are acting under the aegis of the government rather than your own personal legal rights. Ultimately, because of the severity of this type of suit, your satisfaction may be more profound, because you know that your husband not only violated you, but violated society as a whole.

Remember, when filing a civil rights suit, you should consider the fact that it is usually not possible to have the claim covered by homeowners' liability insurance. If your husband is a wealthy man, this will not be a significant consideration. However, if your husband is a middle- to upper-middle-class man, you will want the insurance to pay for your claims, thereby maximizing your final settlement. The reason the insurance company may not have to pay is that most policies exclude coverage for an intentional act by a human being that harms another human being.

There are many subtle distinctions in the law that may enable your lawyer to tiptoe around these elements. For example, suppose that in a drunken argument, your husband drove his car through your house, smashed the wall, and injured you. A jury could assess that your husband's inebriation prevented him from forming the intent to harm you or the house. In such a case, your husband's actions could be considered negligent, which would enable you to receive compensation from the homeowners' liability insurance. Most civil rights violations, however, will be considered as intentional acts and may be excluded from insurance coverage.

Finally, every case will be different and will necessitate a different analysis. A trained lawyer will be able to interpret the distinctions in your particular case and will determine what type of claim to bring against your husband. One thing is certain—Congress has given you strong constitutionally based rights that will help in your divorce if you have been a victim in your marriage.

| *Setting Your Husband Up for Fault*

Today, divorces are granted on the basis of incompatibility or irreconcilable differences. In the past, however, a spouse needed to establish the other spouse's fault in order to have sufficient justification to file for divorce. In most states, fault-based divorce is, for the most part, an issue of the past.

Nevertheless, fault is still relevant in many jurisdictions for many other aspects of divorce—for example, as a factor in determining and awarding maintenance alimony and custody of minor children. The use of fault as a strategic tool can also help persuade your judge that your should receive more in your divorce settlement.

Fault can be established by proving the following:

1. Adultery.
2. Mental abuse and cruelty.
3. Physical abuse.
4. Alcohol or drug abuse.

There are many other grounds which can be used to establish fault. These are simply the most common.

Fault has been statutorily excluded in some jurisdictions, while in others it has been left in a weakened form. Usually, the states that have kept fault in some form allow it to be used as a factor in the court's discretion. The court may use the claim of fault to punish one party in the divorce by making a larger property distribution to the other party. Fault might be used to award more alimony to the wife, but it is particularly used to award custody.

Regardless of whether your state still considers fault, almost all lawyers will attempt to negotiate for an award of an increased share of marital assets by making innuendoes or threats, or using coercion and other legal maneuvers based upon actions of fault by a spouse. No one wants his dirty laundry aired before the court, where it becomes public record.

The appendix in the back of this book lists which states use fault as a basis for obtaining a divorce. Many states use fault and no-fault separately or in concert.

---

*Strategy 27. Use fault against your husband as an additional means to win your divorce.*

---

When you attempt to establish your husband's fault, you must search your memory thoroughly. Surely your husband is at fault for some past indiscretion or instance of abuse. It may be difficult to uncover these memories, as most people tend to forget painful experiences. You must, however, dig carefully through your subconscious memory, no matter how difficult it may be, in order to establish your husband's fault.

Remember, judges are not stupid. If a domestic judge finds any evidence that one spouse has fabricated fault issues in order to be awarded money, the judge will penalize that party. The penalty can be as small as a slap on the hand, or it may be severe. Perhaps the judge will use his discretion to award most of the property to your husband, grant no alimony, and make you pay your own attorney fees. No matter what the decision of the judge is, you will be the loser.

# Adultery

There are many ways that a shrewd wife can catch her husband having an affair, but it requires careful investigation and searching. Furthermore, not all evidence that indicates adulterous behavior will provide a preponderance of the evidence. In other words, a court will require you to prove your claims of adultery.

In order to win, you should have more than one piece of evidence to show to the judge. Keep in mind, however, that many of the signs have reasonable explanations, which will allow your husband to disprove your claim.

Signs of adulterous behavior can be broken down into the categories listed below. Review all of them carefully and prepare a sheet of paper with three headings at the top. Determine how many of these facts are present in your marriage and place them in the appropriate category.

### Substantial Signs of Adultery

1. Lipstick on his collar. This is a highly relevant indication of adultery.
2. Perfume smell on his clothing. This is a less substantial finding than lipstick, but certainly means that your husband has been close to another woman.
3. Love letters from a co-worker or close friend that you find in a secret hiding place at your home, or in your husband's office. These offer definite proof of an affair.
4. Credit card charges that appear on his monthly statement from lingerie establishments or other businesses from which you have not received anything.
5. Florist bills and receipts for flowers purchased for his mistress.

## Probable Signs of Adultery

1. Weekend business travel to romantic locations, or weekend travel to normal business locations out of town that is repeated or seems suspicious.
2. Abnormal cash withdrawals from bank accounts that can be logically charted to show a steady pattern of cash withdrawal. The cash is most probably being given to his mistress for her living expenses.
3. Late evenings out with co-workers whom you have never met or heard of.
4. Phone calls from an unknown person. Pay attention to these, especially when your husband becomes unresponsive when you question him about who called.

## Reasonable Signs of Adultery

1. Third-party hearsay (for example, someone tells you they saw your husband out with another woman).
2. Your husband comes home late and has a plausible explanation for his whereabouts.
3. An old girlfriend calls him to wish him a happy birthday.
4. He comes home from work wearing a different shirt than he had on in the morning when he left home, indicating that he probably had lipstick or perfume on his shirt from a mistress and did not have time to launder the shirt.
5. He stops making love to you, making up excuses for a long period of time.
6. He begins to spend more time with his male buddies and ignores you.

Why do you want to establish adultery on the part of your husband? There may be many reasons. It can help to show that he is at fault in the marriage. His adultery will establish his lack of concern for the family and the children when arguing over custody. Adultery will establish grounds for the judge to consider when determining the equities involved in your case. Evidence of adultery may be the sole factor that tips the scales of justice in your favor.

## Mental Abuse and Cruelty

A claim of mental abuse and cruelty is wide-ranging, with hard-hitting effect. The same theory can be used in your divorce in combination with the marital tort action. In most instances, the use of this claim will provide substantial leverage on your divorce action.

Because some states do not allow this claim to be brought additionally in a separate action for marital torts, you need to consider bringing it as the main cause of action in your divorce case. In the event that the court will not allow the same claim to be brought later, you have not lost the claim altogether.

In legal terms, this issue is a legal matter that concerns whether you can join the divorce action and the marital tort action together, or whether they must be brought separately. Your lawyer will be able to research your state's law deciding this issue. Since the laws are new and changing, this issue may not yet have been decided in your state.

To establish mental abuse and cruelty, you can acquire evidence by many different methods. First, and most logical, is to have the testimony of a witness who has observed the acts of abuse. Your friends, parents, and children can help you with this, but disinterested witnesses are much more credible than witnesses who are close to you, as juries don't believe friends. Once again, you have a civil standard to prove that the claim is more likely to be true than not true, in contrast to a criminal standard of proof beyond a reasonable doubt. The civil standard is much easier to prove in court.

To acquire credible evidence of mental abuse, seek the counsel and treatment of a psychologist who can be called as an expert witness to substantiate your claims. Even though the testimony of the psychologist is one-sided, it is admissible and can be extremely useful in establishing mental abuse.

Another method with which you can establish this claim is to keep a diary or log with dates, times, and a complete summary of abusive statements or acts.

The use of a tape recorder is a particularly good way of proving abuse. However, you should not proceed with tape recording until you have consulted a lawyer regarding the state laws in your jurisdiction. These laws may make tape recording illegal. See the following chapter for more information about tape recording.

Remember, no matter how much evidence you collect, it can never be enough. Always refer to your master plan, and collect as much evidence as you can to bolster your claims.

## Physical Abuse

Establishing physical abuse is a much easier task than proving emotional distress claims. In many states the legislature has created laws for protection from physical abuse. In the event of abuse, the evidence can be documented with photographs. Contacting the police and local abuse hotlines provides additional evidence that can be introduced into testimony.

Many cities and states now have policies that require police to arrest one party in a domestic violence situation. Also, because the signs of physical abuse can disappear over a relatively short period of time, evidence must be established at opportune moments, as the following case history shows.

> Terry had been married to her husband for ten years. Her husband routinely fought with her physically, but never used enough force to leave telltale signs. After speaking with her

lawyer, Terry realized that she needed some type of proof that her husband physically attacked her.

She waited until one night when her husband was out drinking and carousing with his male friends. While he was away, Terry dropped several vases on the floor, smashed a chair and broke it, and kicked a hole in the wall.

When her husband returned, he looked disheveled and was speaking in a slurred manner. Terry immediately began arguing with him in an attempt to get into a fight. Within a few minutes, her husband was angry and out of control, so Terry went into another room and dialed 911. When the operator answered, Terry was already crying because of her husband's rage. The operator could overhear Terry's husband yelling in the background and recorded the call. By the time the police arrived, her husband had calmed down, but the police officer listened to Terry's story, saw the damage to the house, smelled alcohol on her husband's breath, and arrested him. Terry finally had the proof that she needed to win the court's sympathy.

This case illustrates that while photographs of physical injuries are the best evidence to present to the court, police reports can work equally well. To ensure that the law favors your position, be sure that you are the spouse who makes the call to 911. Police often choose to arrest the non-calling spouse when a domestic violence call is made to 911.

A substantial number of cities nationwide have laws or policies requiring that at least one or both spouses be arrested when a 911 call is made for domestic violence. Remember, when battling a divorce, it is often the first person to react who wins the war.

# Alcohol or Drug Abuse

Claiming that your husband abuses alcohol or drugs is a strategy that can be considered somewhat dirty or underhanded, and should only be used as a last resort. People have a right to privacy, and it is only the most devious wife who will use this tactic.

Typically, it is much easier to establish alcohol abuse than drug abuse. One way of doing this is through courtroom testimony of family and friends. However, this testimony is subject to cross-examination, and the credibility of the witnesses will be scrutinized. The judge can use his discretion to determine that a witness is biased because of his or her relation to you.

Remember, divorce judges hear every possible allegation and become hardened to the day-to-day problems of married couples. To convince the judge, you must provide harsh evidence that cannot be blocked out by deafened ears.

Drug abuse is harder to prove, because most individuals are discreet about this type of behavior. If you also use drugs, your husband can make similar accusations against you, especially if your doctor is prescribing Valium or some other tranquilizer. A judge might consider this evidence against you. It could affect not only your settlement, but also your custody fight for the children.

*Strategy 28. Before claiming your husband's alcohol or drug abuse, examine your own usage.*

When a judge hears each of you alleging that the other is a drunk or a drug addict, he will be affected in one of two ways: He may completely disbelieve the allegations, or he may believe that both of you are drug users, in which case he won't feel sorry for either one of you. In either instance, it could hurt your case.

Several other types of evidence can be introduced in court to establish alcohol or drug abuse. Following are most, but not all, evidentiary methods of establishing drug or alcohol abuse.

### Photographic Evidence

This can establish a person's condition at a given time or place. Although a still photo is subject to many interpretations, remember the adage that a picture is worth a thousand words. If you have a photograph of your husband with a drugged or drunken expression on his face, or lying on the floor in a drunken stupor, the judge will be able to use this as hard evidence.

---

*Strategy 29.* *Photographic and videotaped evidence is far better than a live witness.*

---

### Videotaped Evidence

This is much more useful as evidence than a still photograph. Videotape captures the real-life actions of a person and is much less subject to judicial interpretation and discretion. Laws concerning evidence may or may not allow the evidence.

The tricky part is to get your husband to unknowingly submit to the videotaping. If you are at a party, and your husband gets drunk and makes an ass out of himself, videotape the evidence.

### Tape-Recorded Evidence

This can provide auditory evidence of intoxication without a visual image. Again, be cautious in collecting tape-recorded evidence, as many state and federal laws make it a crime to tape-record another individual without their knowledge. Tape recording will be examined in depth in the following chapter.

### Medical and Psychological Evidence

This can be highly beneficial to your case. To use this type of evidence and make it admissible in court, you will need to consult with a mental-health professional. Invite your husband to attend the sessions with you and openly discuss his abuse of alcohol or drugs in front of the therapist. Since the mental-health professional is your counselor and does not have any obligations to your husband under physician-patient privilege, he can openly testify in court and relate oral statements made by your husband. Once again, getting your husband to cooperate and attend the sessions is the difficult part.

Keep in mind that the psychologist will be able to testify on your behalf. At the same time, your husband's lawyer will be able to cross-examine the psychologist to elicit testimony helpful to your husband. Whether this will be helpful or hurtful to you will depend upon how loyal the psychologist is to you. Speaking to the psychologist over an extended period of time will allow you to determine whether he will be supportive or disruptive in the event of his testimony at trial.

Attempting to use your husband's medical and psychological records as evidence is extremely difficult in most cases, but there are certain legal methods of maneuvering around privacy laws. A skillful lawyer will know how to dodge the laws and convince the court that the confidentiality laws are not applicable.

This is often seen in cases where a husband files a countersuit and asserts various claims against his wife. In such a case, the husband becomes the plaintiff and may argue that he was mentally damaged, thereby necessitating an investigation into his prior mental status. When spouses begin combat in a divorce war, they often lose sight of simple logic because they are fighting as hard as possible.

Another good strategy is to force your husband into involuntary alcohol treatment with a court-ordered petition. If you have any credible evidence to establish that your husband drinks, you can get a court to order your husband into the hospital for observation.

Once he is committed, you, your family members, or friends can testify that your husband is a drunk. Also, most treatment centers believe in total abstinence, so even if your husband is only a social drinker, his alcohol intake will still be too high in their estimation. It will be easy to convince them that your husband needs help.

The flip side of the coin is that you might destroy your husband's career, and therefore his ability to make a living and pay alimony. Furthermore, he will probably be unable to get health insurance, and his ability to get life insurance will be greatly reduced. Remember, you may want the benefits of these insurance policies. If you or your children are named as beneficiaries in the event of your husband's death, this type of claim can have disastrous consequences.

### Criminal Arrests and Convictions

These provide the best evidence of alcohol or drug abuse. Convictions for drunken driving, possession of drugs, or drug sales will prove to any court that your husband is the person you claim he is. The court will take judicial notice of the conviction upon a lawyer's request, and a copy of the conviction will be admitted into your case, thereby establishing your claims. Charges of driving while intoxicated, public intoxication, drug possession, or any other criminal violation will provide you with the leverage you need to obtain the divorce, a higher alimony award, custody of your children, and a higher property distribution.

In every divorce case, establishing fault requires a great deal of consideration, particularly if your husband's life will be ruined by your claims. Also keep in mind that your children will still need a father, and that they could be emotionally harmed by the situation. As with all aspects of your divorce, you will need to weigh the potential benefit against the possible damage.

| *Tape-Record Your Husband's Conversations*

In many situations you may have the urge to tape-record your husband's conversations. However, this can be considered a criminal act. This topic will be delved into at considerable length, because you need to make an informed and reasoned decision. Tape-recorded evidence should only be acquired after consultation with a local lawyer in your area to determine the admissibility of this type of evidence. The following information is given to help you understand all of the possible methods of gathering evidence to utilize against your husband in court.

One thing is certain—tape-recorded evidence is significantly better than testimony in court without additional proof. All judges understand and expect that people will lie in court. Because of this, they tend to scrutinize any testimony given by an individual if it is not backed up by additional proof such as written documents, tape-recorded evidence, or photographs. To prevent your testimony from appearing suspect, you need to have additional proof. You can't just appear credible. You must undeniably appear to be telling the truth.

Before tape-recording your husband's conversations, check with your attorney to determine if the act can be considered illegal in your area. If it is, completely ignore the following advice.

---

*Strategy 30.* Never tape-record your husband over the
telephone without first consulting your
divorce lawyer.

---

There is a substantial difference between tape-recording
your husband in person and recording him over the phone.
Whenever you tape-record your husband's conversations over a
home, office, or mobile telephone, it is considered a wiretap.
The issue then becomes whether or not this wiretap is illegal.

## Investigate State and Federal Laws about
## Tape-Recording

The Wiretap Act of the United States Code is a federal law
aimed at making phone wiretapping a criminal act punishable
by criminal fines, penalties, and jail sentences. Certainly, you do
not want to be imprisoned for committing an act that might
assist you in your divorce. Remember, your angry husband
could press criminal charges if he has valid evidence of an illegal wiretap.

Under the Wiretap Act, tape recording electronic conversations can be considered illegal and punishable by a criminal fine
and/or imprisonment. But the Wiretap Act is directed toward
interception of a wire or oral communication *without the con-
sent of at least one party* who engages in the conversation. In
laymen's terms, if you speak to your husband on the phone and
tape-record the conversation, you have consented to the tape
recording, and your actions may not be considered criminal.

On the other hand, if you set up a tape recorder on the
phone when your husband is not talking to you, but is speaking
to some third party such as his mistress, his banker, or his

accountant, this can be considered a criminal activity under the Wiretap Act.

In some states an exception to the criminality of wiretapping has been established. A person can tap an extension phone rather than the actual phone on which the other party is speaking. This requires an eavesdropper's presence, or the use of an electrical device that is voice activated and will come on automatically when your husband picks up the other phone.

An exception exists if any given state or federal court chooses to find the Wiretap Act inapplicable in certain circumstances. Again, you must consult your attorney to know for certain if your state is one of the states where these exceptions exist, as some courts find an exception for an extension phone while others do not.

Several state courts have established that domestic situations in divorce matters warrant certain exceptions. Essentially, the courts have declared that the Wiretap Act does not apply when family members in a divorce are tape-recording one another. The purpose of the Wiretap Act is to protect people under the Fourth Amendment Search and Seizure clause. Supposedly, family members cannot expect the same level of privacy. There are several legal cases in which no violation of the Wiretap Act has occurred because the recording was done by family members within the home. Once again, you are cautioned to speak with an attorney in your area, who will research the law and advise you properly.

There are very few courts in which evidence recorded by a spouse is admissible. You must have the advice of legal counsel to determine if your state prohibits this type of evidence. Do not tape-record your spouse over a phone before you speak to an attorney.

Furthermore, there is a distinction between taping a telephone conversation and taping a personal, face-to-face conversation. The personal conversation is not protected by law, while tape-recording your husband over the telephone may be protected, making such recording a criminal act.

Another avenue for determining what law is applicable is to speak to a local state prosecutor's office. The state prosecutor should be familiar with the possible prosecutions of violations of any wiretap law. He or she may provide advice free of charge, while others will say they cannot advise you.

Be careful in choosing the lawyer with whom you speak. Ask for proof of their knowledge, as lawyers tend to be lazy. He may think he knows the right answer, or he may give you his opinion off the top of his head. Question him thoroughly and have him explain how the Wiretap Act affects his opinion. Some lawyers will not be familiar with the Wiretap Act and will have to research the law to provide you with an accurate legal opinion. There are many good, knowledgeable, competent lawyers who will take the time to review the law to advise you properly, but finding these lawyers can be difficult.

Laws surrounding wiretapping are not only vague, but difficult to find. You must have your lawyer check the federal, state, and city laws so he or she can determine if you are violating one or all of them. Because of the obscurity of these laws, it is highly important to have a criminal lawyer, rather than a domestic lawyer, inquire into the matter. Criminal lawyers are accustomed to analyzing laws in cases where their criminal clients are charged with a crime and the prosecutor has tape-recorded their conversations.

## Install a Home Tape-Recording Device

If you are going to go to the trouble of tape-recording your husband, do it right! Tape-record him as he is talking to his mistress, when he is drunk and abusive, while he is screaming and cursing at your children, or when he brags of his wealth. This can be accomplished secretly so that he doesn't know until it is too late.

## Tape-Record Your Husband's Conversations

Several mechanisms have been developed for tape-recording purposes and can be obtained through various outlets. These mechanisms come in all shapes and sizes and with different capabilities. You can consult with your attorney, who may be able to direct you to these sources, or you may simply be able to find one in the phone book. The following is a list of the various devices which you can purchase.

1. Voice-activated telephone suction device with tape recorder. This device will stay inoperative until its computer chip detects a voice to tape-record. You will not run out of tape quickly, because the machine only tape-records when it recognizes a human voice speaking.

2. Voice-activated telephone recording device with modular connection and voice activation. This device will plug into an available telephone outlet on the same telephone line. It will automatically turn on when it detects voice or sound. With this device, you are actually plugged into the phone line, which makes it much more confidential. The suction device, in contrast, cannot simply be hidden. It needs to be on an active line where someone has the handset picked up to overhear the conversation.

3. Dish-type listening device with tape recorder. This eavesdropping device looks like a small satellite receiving dish and can be pointed in the direction of a conversation from far away. Earphones are attached with an amplifier to increase the sound the dish hears. The individual will be unable to detect that his conversation is being secretly recorded. You can set up across the street or at greater distances depending upon the type of unit you purchase.

Perhaps your husband routinely has conversations from your home that concern his financial affairs. Or perhaps he is gutsy enough to speak with his mistress from the home telephone. A secret voice-activated tape recording device will provide all the information you need. Even if the tape recording is not admissible, you may learn enough about his financial dealings to point your divorce lawyer in the right direction to discover his hidden assets.

Be careful in gathering evidence of this type, as it can backfire on you. If your husband finds out about your chicanery and determines that a violation of law has occurred, he may turn you in to local authorities. Keep in mind that sometimes the gain is not worth the ultimate consequences. You must use your own discretion to determine which way to proceed.

## Carry a Concealed Tape Recorder

Safety from prosecution is more probable if you are able to tape one-on-one conversations with your husband. Suppose your husband has such a bad temper that you know you will eventually have a perfect opportunity to capture his rage. If you carry a concealed tape recorder on your person or in your purse, his next violent outburst will be recorded for posterity. When you tell the judge your husband is an atrocious, loud-mouthed bully, the judge will have no choice but to believe you after you play the tape.

If your husband was drunk and became verbally abusive, he will deny his behavior later in court. He will dress in the appropriate conservative attire and will appear professional, thereby presenting to the judge an exemplary façade. The judge will then doubt your claims of abuse based on your husband's appearance. And remember, judges become hardened to individuals lying about their spouses in a divorce. They often disregard the truth because it sounds like the same old story. With so many falsehoods, judges cannot always be expected to know the truth. This time, however, will be different—you will have concrete proof.

You can acquire this proof with the following devices.

1. Disguised pen with miniature tape-recording device. This product will allow you to carry a pen in a pocket and tape-record your husband, his accountant, his financial advisor, or any other individual who is privy to relevant evidence that can be used in your divorce. Your husband will never know he is being tape-recorded in your presence. You have consented to the tape-recording as one party to the conversation, which in most instances will make it perfectly legal.

2. Briefcase with microphone and tape recorder. Unless you normally carry a briefcase, this will be too obtrusive and look abnormal.

3. Camouflaged tape-recording devices. Many other tape-recording devices have been developed that can fit in your purse or look like an object that seems ordinary to the casual observer.

Tape-recorded evidence, if admissible, will prove your claims and allegations beyond all reasonable doubt, although in a civil divorce you don't even need such strong proof. You simply have to prove that your claims are more likely true than not. Tape-recorded evidence will more than meet this lesser evidentiary burden.

Patricia claimed her husband was verbally abusive and called her a whore and other vile names. Her husband was an investment banker and always appeared to be the perfect gentleman. However, when he was drinking and alone with Patricia, he let his true character emerge. He would shout and threaten her for hours upon end. But when the couple was in public his abusive behavior never surfaced. He was wise enough to protect himself. His rationale was that if no one else heard it, then it could not be proven and certainly must not be true. However, Patricia was cagey enough to buy an eavesdropping device to prove that her husband abused her. Over a period of time he called her every name in the book. He accused her of affairs that she did not have and told her that he would destroy her life if she filed for divorce. He insisted that she would end up with nothing, and even went to the extent of telling her that he would stop paying for the education of their children and would not send any of the children to college if she filed for divorce.

When the time came to discuss property settlement, Patricia informed her husband of the tapes. Ultimately, they were never admitted into court, but because the husband and his lawyer heard the tapes, the husband caved in and was forced to pay Patricia every penny she demanded. Her husband even agreed to pay college expenses for the children, even though the court could not have forced him to pay for child support past the age of eighteen. Without the taped evidence, Patricia's property settlement and child support payments would have been substantially less.

This case history underscores a critical point: Verbal allegations without any hard evidence to substantiate them lead to a loss in court. But the same verbal allegations with a tape recording to back them up will leave the court in little doubt concerning their credibility.

Do you want to win or lose in the game of matrimonial war? If winning is your goal, arm yourself appropriately. Otherwise, don't play a game that you are not tactically equipped to win.

In Patricia's case, the tapes' admissibility in court never became an issue, because Patricia's husband and his lawyer did not want to risk that the court might admit them. As is the case with most husbands, he did not want to take the risk of having his worst actions brought before the court.

Remember, tape-recorded evidence is just one more weapon you can place in your arsenal for fighting the divorce war.

# Chapter 13 | *Use a Private Investigator*

Although divorces today are granted simply on the basis of incompatibility or irreconcilable differences and fault need not be established, proving your husband's fault can benefit you in other ways. Fault is still considered by many courts when determining whom to award custody of the children, how much alimony will be paid, or which spouse should get the home.

Community property states rely upon fault evidence to a much lesser degree than equitable distribution states. Nevertheless, it will only augment your case if you establish before the court that your husband is an abusive, alcoholic philanderer who deserves to relinquish all of his money to you.

You can establish this by presenting hard evidence to the court in the form of tape-recorded conversations, written documents, or photographs. Additionally, you can have the oral testimony of a witness or detective to substantiate your version of any marital situation. By hiring a detective, you can acquire hard evidence that will help convince the judge that you not only should win your case, but also should get more in the final settlement.

Perhaps in reviewing your case, the judge sees both your own and your husband's sides of the situation equally, and his or her first inclination is to distribute the settlement evenly between you. In such a case, no unusually substantial award will be given to either party, as no negative facts have been established for or against you or your husband. If, however, you are able to present the judge with a significant body of evidence against your husband, he or she may decide in your favor. With some investigation and forethought, you can obtain the evidence that will ultimately help you win your case.

You can prove many facts in your favor by using a detective who might be able to photograph evidence of an affair. For example, take the classic television or movie scenario in which a detective pops into a motel room and snaps a photograph of a husband in bed with another woman. This really does occur. Your detective can provide you with undeniable photographic proof of your husband's infidelity. As the adage goes, a picture is worth a thousand words. In a divorce case, the sleazier the picture, the better. If you show your husband at his worst, his subsequent denials in court will not be believed. Any negative evidence will help tip the scales of justice towards you and away from your husband.

Matrimonial lawyers still love to use the fault concept to prove that their client has unwittingly been betrayed and is absolutely faultless. Lawyers know that judges can be influenced and made to feel sympathetic toward a party in a divorce case. When a judge is presented with fault-based evidence, his or her sympathies may enter into play and will influence the decision to award child support, alimony, and property distribution.

Even if the law in your state does not take fault into consideration, the judge will not forget the photographic image. It will be carved indelibly into his or her mind. Once any negative evidence is seen or heard, it is not easily forgotten.

Suppose you are attempting to show that your husband routinely gets drunk and stays out chasing other women. A detective can follow your husband, photograph him where he hangs out, and establish a pattern of misconduct over a period of time. Sure, you could get up on the stand and tell the judge your story about how terrible your husband is. But it will be much better to prove your husband's bad behavior through photographic evidence combined with testimony from the detective. Strong evidence helps render a strong verdict in your favor. The advantage of photographic evidence is that even if it is not admissible, the judge will hear your lawyer argue that the photographs should be admitted. When the judge makes his or her final decision, the mental images of what the photos might have conveyed will be stuck in his or her mind. You win either way.

An additional advantage is that your detective can also uncover financial assets by performing record searches that can help your lawyer gather evidence to prove your husband's wealth. If the detective finds only one additional asset to show the judge, it is still one more asset for you to claim.

# Find a Private Investigator Who Knows the Divorce Game

Finding a detective who is skilled in developing matrimonial cases is difficult. Most, if not all, detectives are not really as competent as the glamorized sleuths in the movies. If you hire the wrong detective, you may lose your case.

As bad as some lawyers are, most detectives are worse. A safe estimate of the percentage of detectives who are worth hiring is probably in the range of five to ten percent. The remainder are simply inexperienced, lazy, or inept.

Your divorce lawyer may already have a favored detective who has helped prepare cases many times before. If so, rely upon your lawyer's recommendation. Past performance records provide excellent indicators for future performance.

*Strategy 31.* Hire a detective who specializes in matrimonial investigation.

If your lawyer does not have a detective to recommend, then consider all of the factors below to determine whether or not the detective is right for you.

### Factor 1
Investigate the experience level of the detective, including the length of career, type of detection, and percentage of cases dealing with matrimonial law. Ask for the detective's percentage of wins. Get specific case names, and check out the court file to see if the detective lied to you. If the detective says he or she has a one hundred percent win record, you know he or she is lying. No detective wins one hundred percent of the time. Look for a detective who is at least in the seventy-five percent win category.

### Factor 2
Find out how many divorce lawyers in your city use the detective. The more, the better. Call the lawyers up and inquire about the detective's ability, reputation, and other attributes.

### Factor 3
Determine how many times the detective has testified in depositions or trial. You don't want some kid who is wet behind the ears. A good detective won't be manipulated on the stand by your husband's lawyer.

### Factor 4

Does the detective have an aversion to obtaining photographic and electronically recorded evidence? Believe it or not, some detectives do. Stay away from these.

### Factor 5

Is the detective articulate? A detective who is not well-spoken can hurt your case. You need a detective who can paint an accurate and compelling picture.

### Factor 6

What level of education and experience does the detective have? Some detectives are college-educated or have prior long-term careers with police agencies, the FBI or other government organizations. Prior law-enforcement experience will usually make for a better detective. If your detective received a GED after dropping out of high school, he or she will most likely be of little help to you.

### Factor 7

Does he or she have a nice appearance that will impress the court, or an appearance that may detract from his or her credibility? A clean-cut, professional image is what you should look for. Courts are ultraconservative. A detective with a pony tail or shabby clothes will be much less credible.

### Factor 8

What will the detective charge? Some detectives will rack up a bill for wasted time. You want a detective who charges only for actual time spent on your case. Inquire at the outset as to the estimated charges for the case. Ask for an estimate in writing, and obtain hourly fee and expense charges in writing.

By considering all of the factors above you should be able to locate a detective who is right for you.

## Pay the Investigator with Your Husband's Money

Always find a way to spend your husband's money to pay for your detective, as even the smallest case can result in a bill for thousands of dollars. Pay the detective's retainer in cash withdrawn from your husband's accounts, and be sure that you obtain a written estimate of time and expenses that shows a credit against the retainer. Take a cash advance against your husband's credit cards for subsequent bills for the detective's time.

---

*Strategy 32.* *Hire a detective to prove your husband has a bad character, and pay for the services with your husband's money.*

---

Do not write a check to the detective. A personal check, cashier's check, or money order is a permanent record that can be traced. If the evidence turns out contrary to your allegations, you will have created proof against your case. You don't want this type of evidence to come into court and back up your husband's defense. Pay in cash, ask for a receipt, and hide the receipts where no one can find them.

Keep any evidence of the detective's employment quietly hidden until the appropriate time, when you can spring the detective's evidence upon your unsuspecting husband.

---

*Strategy 33.* *When you hire a detective, do not pay him by check. Keep his knowledge and existence confidential.*

---

## Use a Private Investigator

Strategy in your divorce is one of your most important weapons. Strategy involves creating a logical, reasoned plan, implementing the plan, and then proving the planned objectives before the court. The more hard evidence you can establish with your detective, the easier winning your divorce will be. The right detective will be able to help you implement your plan, and may augment it with ideas of his own.

However, don't divulge your plan to the detective. Only discuss what you believe to be true and enlist his help in establishing this truth. Once the detective is on your side, you will be able to produce the solid evidence that will seal your victory.

# Chapter 14 | *Avoid Evidence That Can Be Used Against You*

One of the most serious errors you can make in creating and implementing your divorce plan is to create evidence that will come back to haunt you. Many women who are planning a divorce fail to consider a judge's power to award them *nothing*. If your judge determines that you are wrong or that you have lied in court, you could lose everything.

If your husband can actually furnish evidence that proves that you have set him up, the result can be disastrous. Your judge will recognize your trickery, and your well-established plan will backfire, leaving you with few assets or nothing at all. To avoid this, you must develop a well-thought-out plan that remains absolutely confidential.

## Do Not Talk When You Can Be Tape-Recorded

Remember, if you don't tell anyone about your plan, there is no way to prove its existence unless it has been written down. Your husband may be savvy enough to talk with you and lead you into revealing your schemes. If he tape-recorded your conversation without your knowledge, the judge will hear the tape, and your plan will be exposed.

Even if you believe your husband is an incompetent, uncaring, boring human being, he may still have the foresight to protect himself. Once he recognizes any sign of your disloyalty, beware!

If your husband is perceptive, he will become aware of your purpose long before the divorce action arises. If he has been married previously, the knowledge gained from his prior divorce action will give him an advantage. He will already know some of the tactics people use when seeking a divorce. He will be much more suspicious than a husband going through divorce proceedings for the first time.

---

*Strategy 34. Never verbalize anything that you do not want repeated in court.*

---

If you said something unwise and it has been tape-recorded, you will pay dearly for it later.

## Do Not Reveal Your Plan to Anyone

Nothing is sacred when it comes to divorce. Friends can turn on you. Even your best friend might be sleeping with your husband, especially if he has money.

For example, if your husband becomes aware of your plan, he may convince one of your most loyal and trusted friends to assist him. Perhaps he will offer money, sex, or other incentives to enlist your friend's help. Your friend may convince you that she has only one desire—to help you destroy your husband. You will then dutifully outline every detail of your plan for divorce. But unknown to you, she may secretly tape-record your discussion of the plan, and turn the tape over to your husband's lawyer. If any such scenario occurs, you will lose.

Perhaps you are having a secret affair that you plan to continue following the divorce. Once again, you tell your loyal best friend about Alfredo, the tennis coach at your country club. Guess what? She tape-records you and delivers the tape to your husband.

Once she has betrayed you without your knowledge, you will be the one on the defensive, and your husband can play you like a concert piano. He can make it appear that you were the wicked one.

---

*Strategy 35.* *Never trust anyone else. This includes your mother, sister, best friend, and divorce lawyer. Shocking as it may seem, any one of them could betray you.*

---

# Do Not Write Down Your Plan

Never write down anything about your plan. Written evidence of any type in your handwriting or with your signature will be detrimental to your goals. People have a tendency to act without thinking of the consequences, thereby creating written evidence against themselves. Criminal lawyers encounter this problem regularly. You may recall the married couple who were spies for the CIA and became turncoat double agents for the Soviet Union. When their house was raided, written evidence of their bank accounts holding $2.4 million in earnings from Soviet sources was found, as were lists of their activities. This written documentation furnished sufficient evidence to bring a sentence of life imprisonment for the husband.

When you write down any detail of your plan, you do nothing but harm yourself. Even a simple outline of your strategy, or scratch notes that may be interpreted as calculations of your husband's wealth, will be enough to establish your intentions. It is imperative that you avoid writing down anything that may later be construed as an attempt to formulate a strategy.

---

*Strategy 36.* *Never write down your plan or keep any written documentation that might establish a plan's existence.*

---

The following case history will further illuminate this very critical point.

Prior to filing for divorce, Eve created a plan and wrote down an outline with step-by-step instructions on how to carry out and finalize her strategy. She hid these plans in a jewelry box in a secret compartment. Unfortunately, however, her husband was aware of this compartment. One day when Eve was out of the house, he found her written notes and outline. He immediately rushed to his divorce lawyer, filed for divorce, and attached a copy of the notes as evidence of her mischievous intent.

In the temporary orders issued by the court, Eve was given little more than her car, along with the payments still due on it. She lost everything else. In the end, nothing could be said in her defense to convince the judge that she deserved any compensation for her marriage, and no permanent award of alimony was provided. Ultimately, her husband walked away the winner of the divorce without paying so much as one dollar for Eve's attorney fees.

# Do Not Admit to Your Plan in Deposition or Court

Assuming that you have skillfully avoided being tape-recorded or caught with written notes of your plan, you should not have any problem once the lawsuit is on file. However, you will have your deposition taken under oath and must still be concerned with being found out at trial. Many of the lawyers in the field of matrimonial law handle thousands of divorces over their careers and will be experienced enough to recognize factors indicating that the husband has been set up.

Once your husband's attorney recognizes this, he will spend hour upon hour attempting to evidence the plan by scrutinizing your testimony and actions for errors. Your husband's lawyer will submit written interrogatories that require you to respond truthfully with sworn testimony, and your answers can be used against you later.

The only protection you have against this is your lawyer's ability to object to the questions asked of you. If he loses his objection, you have to testify and will still be compelled to answer the interrogatories by court order. Your lawyer should be an adept, skilled trial lawyer in order to help protect you from your husband's lawyer. Ultimately, the war will become a war between lawyers as much as a war between spouses.

---

*Strategy 37.* *Without question, hire the sharpest, most intelligent, skilled trial attorney who also handles matrimonial law.*

---

Many skilled trial lawyers will simply refuse to handle a divorce case, because defending them repeatedly often becomes boring. The best trial lawyers will become specialized in other areas of the law and will only handle the most lucrative divorce cases. If they take on a divorce case, they command exorbitant hourly rates.

Nevertheless, it is imperative that you hire the best lawyer that money can buy in order to win. The lawyer's skill in trying your case, defending your position, and revealing as little evidence as possible to the other side may be the single most important weapon in your divorce case.

# Chapter 15 | *In Divorce Negotiations, Start High and Negotiate Down*

Failing to negotiate properly is a major downfall of most lawyers. With this in mind, you should make sure that you are fully equipped to negotiate effectively. No one expects a client to be skilled in negotiations but, by following the advice in this chapter, you can surprise everyone and increase your chances of receiving a higher settlement.

## Ask for More Than You Expect

In a divorce situation, no one ever gets as much as they ask for. You must realize from the outset of your negotiations that your expectations of what you should receive in the divorce are far more grand than what you may actually get. Once you have come to understand this basic principle of domestic law, you can easily see why you should always request more than you expect to receive.

---

*Strategy 38.* *Always ask for more than what is fair, and substantially more than you think you deserve.*

---

Husbands expect to be financially stung in their divorce, and very often they are. It is a rare occasion where the husband walks away from the divorce with more than he had before the legal suit took place. Men are occasionally able to make a claim against their wives for alimony or child support or property distribution. They rarely do get alimony, but an award of child support is becoming a more common occurrence. For your husband to come out ahead, he would have to receive a portion of your premarital assets owned before the marriage and/or alimony.

Remember, your husband expects to pay—his divorce lawyer told him he would—and now you have the opportunity to make this a reality.

How much you receive in a settlement depends upon the financial status of your husband, whether you have children, how long you have been married, and other relevant facts about your marriage. If you have signed a prenuptial contract, this will severely limit what you can ask for and receive in the final outcome.

One thing is certain: you won't receive anything simply because of your husband's generosity. In order to get as much as possible in your settlement, you have to ask for everything.

Remember that your husband is afraid of how much he will lose in the divorce. He fears the highest possible award in your favor. You can use this to your advantage. The greater your husband's fear, the greater the possibility that he will offer to settle graciously with the hope of keeping his remaining assets.

You can always reduce your request for money, but once you set your lowest limit you have played out your hand. If your husband knows that you will settle for one year of alimony instead of ten, he has absolutely no incentive to offer you any additional amount. Fear of the unknown is the weapon you can utilize to make your husband conform to your wishes.

# Request Everything

When asking for your fair share of the marital assets, you need to itemize every conceivable piece of property. The shrewd, wealthy husband may have hundreds of thousands of dollars concealed from his wife. He will have overseas bank accounts and real estate holdings that are barely traceable. He may maintain stocks, bank accounts, or other financial holdings in the name of a relative and have all relevant documentation sent to another address.

If the asset does not require reporting to the IRS on an annual basis, he will be able to hide it much more easily. Cash, gold coins, platinum, silver, and many other monetary instruments are not detectable.

With this in mind, you should look into the holdings of his stock portfolios. Does he hold stocks, bonds, or funds in overseas ventures that he does not report to the IRS? You should be savvy enough to look for proof of your husband's overseas business dealings.

If he owns his own business, what holdings does the business have? What is its worth? Remember, because these determinations are subjective, different experts might value the business at different levels. Many wives have had the misfortune of allowing their husbands to keep their businesses, thinking they were only worth the book value shown on a balance sheet. However, if your husband's business is profitable, it will have inherent value for its longevity, its good standing in the community, and its ability to generate income. A sale of the business might easily bring twice its gross sales, even though it only shows a ten percent profit. This is because buyers normally purchase a prospective business on its ability to generate future revenue. The only way to be sure of the value of the business is to hire an expert to evaluate its true fair market value.

Artwork is another personal asset that may be subject to various opinions on value. An expert opinion is a must. Find the right expert who will know the true value of the artwork. You and your husband may have bought an art piece for a small amount of money several years ago, but that does not mean the art has not risen in value.

Don't forget coin collections or other rare artifacts. The value of rarities can be surprisingly high. Remember, men tend to conceal the truth about their worth or the worth of any given asset. If your husband told you that his 1962 Ferrari is worth one hundred thousand dollars, it might actually be worth two million one hundred thousand dollars.

Have an expert value every single piece of property, whether it is personal property or real estate. Never rely on your husband's estimates of the value of the property.

## Overestimate the Fair Market Value of Your Husband's Assets

As previously noted, valuation of your marital assets is subject to judicial discretion. This means, quite frankly, that a flip of a coin might decide the value of your car, a collection, or a boat. If you make the mistake of testifying about the fair market value of your property without the aid of an expert appraiser, you risk taking a big loss. There are appraisers for almost every type of property imaginable, and you can utilize this diversity by getting every piece of property evaluated.

Your husband will find an appraiser who will testify to the lowest value of all of his property holdings. You, on the other hand, need an appraiser who will testify to the highest potential value. The court will then have to decide whether to believe the high estimate or the low estimate. More often than not, the court will split the two valuations, believing that both are unrealistic.

Finally, never tell the court what you believe to be the actual value of any asset. Your chosen appraiser will inflate the value of an asset, thereby providing you with another strategic weapon.

# Find Experts Who Will Testify for You

Experts or appraisers are affectionately called "prostitutes" in the legal profession, as lawyers, judges, clerks, and other legally knowledgeable people are aware that testimony can be bought. Even experts with the qualifications to appear credible will only continue to get work if they testify favorably for the attorneys or clients paying them. An expert who is fair and just is an expert without work.

As a result of this unusual concept of justice, opportunities exist for experts, or prostitutes, to convey their opinions in court. Experts are a necessary evil when fighting a divorce war. Fighting without them can result in your defeat.

Education is an important factor to consider when making your decision to hire an expert. Supposedly, the more educated the expert is, the more likely the court will choose to believe his or her testimony.

If the expert has testified before your judge in the past and has appeared credible, it will strengthen the judge's impression of his or her testimony in your case. Did the expert win before this judge in the past, or did another expert beat him out? You must know their win-loss records in order to pick the right one.

Your divorce lawyer will know which experts are favorable to him. An astute, knowledgeable expert who is on your lawyer's payroll will be certain to know which side his bread is buttered on.

Be certain that your expert has the credentials to back up his opinions. If he values real estate, does he have education and experience in the appraisal of real estate? Or, if the expert evaluates automotive collections, does he have a specialized knowledge of rare automobiles?

Perhaps your case is one which requires a bevy of experts for a total valuation. In such a situation, one expert will not be sufficient. If your marital assets are large, several experts will have to be utilized, because no one is a jack-of-all-trades. A divorce judge will tend to view the opinions of an expert who appraises too many types of property as frivolous.

Most importantly, if you are attempting to value your husband's business, you don't want an accountant or CPA to do the valuation. They tend to look at the book value or depreciated value of assets, rather than the creative value. That is to say, the value of a business or property is only limited by the amount that a willing buyer will pay to a willing seller. Your husband, on the other hand, will want an accountant to prove to the court how little a business or asset is worth in only accounting terms.

---

*Strategy 39.* *Always hire an expert who will stand by your side of the case.*

---

If you hire an expert with less credibility than your husband's expert, you may lose. Find out through your lawyer which expert your husband's lawyer will use, and then begin your shopping for an expert who is more educated, more credible, and most of all, better acquainted with the judge in your case.

Pat had been married for twenty-seven years to a man who owned a large manufacturing company. Her husband's holdings included bank accounts in the Cayman Islands and vast collections. His automobile collection included several Ferraris, two Rolls-Royces, and many other fine vintage motor vehicles.

# In Divorce Negotiations, Start High and Negotiate Down

Pat refused to believe her husband would lie about the value of his financial holdings. She used her trusted family CPA to value both her own holdings and her husband's. However, she failed to take into consideration the fact that her husband would continue paying the accountant's salary after the divorce.

At trial, the CPA testified that the manufacturing company was only worth its book value of one and a half million dollars. (The company was sold three years later for its true value of eight million dollars.) His car collection was valued at only ten percent of its actual value. The CPA also withheld information about bank accounts outside of the U.S.

All in all, Pat came out with a substantial settlement of around six hundred thousand dollars. But had the true value been known and testified to, Pat would have been entitled to almost five million dollars.


Alice was married to a husband who was in middle management and considered middle-class. He did not have a great amount of wealth to split in the divorce. They had a house, one rental property, the usual personal property that couples own, and two cars. Their savings were less than two thousand dollars and were easy to divide.

When it came time to divorce, Alice decided she did not want to stay in the marital residence. She and her husband agreed they would each have the property appraised, and then split the two appraisers' values by averaging them. The same was true for the rental property. Alice's husband intended to take out a second mortgage to pay her off in the divorce.

Their home had been owned seventeen years. The rental property had been owned eight years. Alice hired an appraiser who was known for overestimating the value of real estate. Her husband hired a normal appraiser without checking his credentials.

Real estate can be valued many different ways when under appraisal. After Alice's appraiser provided his report, he produced computer profiles and comparisons that justified the value he determined. On the other hand, Alice's husband's appraiser came in at the normal fair market value.

Alice's appraisals came in $55,000.00 higher than her husband's appraisal. Her appraiser helped her obtain an additional $27,500.00 over what she would have received with a normal appraiser.

# Chapter 16

# Finding a Psychologist to Testify Against Your Husband

To ensure that you win your divorce, you will need a psychologist who will act as a counselor, friend, expert, and sword. Finding a psychologist is important not only in child custody matters, but can also be critical in presenting claims for property distribution and alimony. Psychological testimony provides the added credibility that your case requires, as opposing testimony leaves substantial room for the judge's discretion to lean either way.

By hiring the expert who will prove in court that you are the better parent, or an abused spouse, or that you simply deserve an abundance of your husband's assets, you can more easily secure your future.

## Seek Counseling with a Psychologist Who Testifies

While searching for a psychologist, you should look for one who is not only compassionate and caring, but who will reasonably arrive at opinions to back you up in court. Ideally, he or she should be fearless of court.

Seek counseling early in the game to establish the long-term counseling that is needed. If you see the psychologist for only a short period of time, the court will place much less credence in his or her opinion.

Find a psychologist who appears professional and is well-spoken. If the psychologist is not articulate (and many are not), it will damage your case.

Furthermore, psychological experts are no different from the experts discussed in the preceding chapter. They will sell their professional opinions and testify for one side or the other. You want an expert who will back your case up, no matter how strongly he or she is cross-examined by your husband's lawyer.

Even if you had an affair with a younger man, spent all of your husband's money on presents for your boyfriend, and are entirely at fault, you need a psychologist who will say that your behavior was acceptable and justified. A good psychologist will go to the grave backing up your case.

Many people believe psychology is nothing more than professional mumbo jumbo that involves only subjective opinions. However, if your counselor's psychological opinions are based on accurate facts that support the diagnosis and stand up to the scrutiny of the divorce judge, his or her testimony will enable you to win. You want your psychologist to compellingly persuade the judge that you should win the divorce and be awarded the marital assets.

## Find Psychologists Who Do Forensic Work

Psychologists who do forensic work are better suited to help you win your divorce, as they specialize in the application of psychology in legal matters. Simply knowing psychology may not be enough. If the psychologist understands how the legal rules apply to your case, he or she will be better able to support you.

***Strategy 40.*** *Hire the best psychologist you can find.*

The best part about obtaining counseling is that you can get your husband to pay for it. You can chat with your shrink and call your husband every conceivable name in the book, and your husband will unwittingly foot the bill for each session. Perhaps the doctor's fee of $150 per hour is not enough. You might even suggest paying a little extra for the counseling. What could be better? You will have the satisfaction of knowing that your husband is paying for his own character assassination.

Use your discretion, however, when spending marital assets on a psychologist. It's one thing if your husband will pay for it or your insurance company will cover the cost. When the fees are coming out of the marital pie to be divided, be careful not to waste the assets needlessly.

Other women who have gone through a divorce will be able to suggest good psychologists. These wives have already found psychologists who have successfully helped them prove that their husbands are scoundrels. You can use their efforts and experience to your advantage.

Find the psychologist whose clients have won the most money in their divorces. That reputation is a good indicator of that psychologist's ability to help you.

Does the psychologist specialize in abused wives or child custody battles? If so, he or she might have expertise that will be of the utmost benefit to you.

Utilizing the testimony of a psychologist with credibility before the eyes of the court will bolster your valid claims. The doctor can testify about the abuse you have undergone. Abuse may be physical or it may be verbal. Some implied conduct can be considered abuse. Even silence may be considered to be abuse in the right situation. Suppose your husband ignores you and refuses to talk to you as a way of punishment. Perhaps he ignores you for hours or days in order to upset you. There are hundreds of different types of conduct that can be construed as abuse. Only a psychologist trained in this area will be able to conclusively establish why you have been treated unfairly. His testimony will provide the added leverage you need to convince the court to tip the scales of justice in your favor.

Remember, battered-wife syndrome can be induced by verbal abuse. Surely your husband has verbally abused you at some point in your life. Perhaps he told you that you were fat or stupid, or attacked you in some other manner. The psychologist can pinpoint these attacks and arrive at a reasonable diagnosis.

Finally, never for one minute forget your objective: to be rid of your husband, to live in wealth and style, to make your husband pay, and to be the winner in your divorce. The expert forensic psychologist will help you achieve these goals.

The following are criteria for hiring the right professional psychologist.

1.  The psychologist has strong ties to the domestic judge on your case.
2.  The psychologist has testified as an expert in divorce cases in your judicial district and has been qualified as an expert before the courts in that district.
3.  The psychologist has a professional appearance. Avoid the male mental-health counselor who wears a ponytail and earring.
4.  The psychologist is articulate.
5.  The psychologist has an established relationship with your attorney. Your lawyer will know in which direction the counselor leans.
6.  The psychologist is compassionate, sympathetic, and empathetic to your situation.
7.  The psychologist has counseled other wealthy and middle-class women in your city and aided them in

receiving large alimony and property settlement awards.

8.  The psychologist specializes in counseling women suffering from battered-wife syndrome.

9.  The psychologist specializes in counseling women suffering from post-traumatic stress disorder and from situational depression and/or major depression arising from an abusive relationship.

10. The psychologist has a good understanding of the legal system and its application to his counseling.

# Do Not Reveal Your Real Plan to the Psychologist

Even though you are going to find a psychologist who is just as determined as you are, you will always want to conceal your plan. Don't let the psychologist know what you are up to. Rehearse your plan only to yourself. Persuade the psychologist to believe in your case, and make him think that every single fact you give him is a fact he can use as your advocate.

Most psychologists want to believe their patients; there is a strong tendency in mental-health counselors to believe the assertions of a patient until they are disproved. Still, never let down your guard, even if questioned by your psychologist. The moment your doctor loses faith in your case, you will have created a problem of dramatic proportions.

> Amy sought the counseling of a well-known male psychologist and regularly met with him throughout the eight months prior to her divorce. During this time, she was extremely careful to conceal any details of her plan for divorce.
>
> Each week she elaborated on her husband's infidelity and abusive, alcoholic behavior. She told her doctor that her husband would come home early in the morning, with lipstick on his collar and smelling of perfume.

Everything seemed to go well with the counseling. The psychologist would certainly testify on Amy's behalf, and point out to the court that she needed several years of rehabilitative alimony to help her get back on her feet while overcoming the trauma of her marriage.

However, a problem arose a few months into the counseling—she and the psychologist began having an affair.

Amy's husband, who was not actually having an affair, suspected that Amy and the psychologist were sleeping together. He hired a detective to prove his suspicions. The detective followed Amy to her appointments for only a few weeks, but after this relatively short period of surveillance, he was able to photograph Amy at a local motel with the doctor.

The husband's lawyer did not provide proof of the affair to Amy's lawyer until it came time for the trial and cross-examination of the psychologist on the stand. It was all the proof necessary to destroy Amy's case and the credibility of her psychologist.

Ultimately, Amy walked out of the divorce with little more than her clothes and personal possessions.

The moral of this case history is clear. Do not establish strong emotional ties with your experts.

*Strategy 41.* *Always maintain a business relationship with your psychologist and other experts.*

**Chapter 17** | *Strategies for Courtroom Testimony*

As trivial and shallow as it may seem, your appearance in the courtroom will have a substantial impact on the outcome of your case. The judge who presides over your divorce will be influenced not only by your behavior and general disposition, but also by your clothes, hair, jewelry, and makeup.

Your personal style may have an effect in your professional and social life, but in the courtroom it is absolutely critical—it can decide your fate. A judge cannot help but be swayed by your outward appearance. While this may seem to go against the principles of courtroom justice, it is an inevitable reality.

Appearance has such a dramatic effect in the courtroom that a whole new breed of expert has evolved in response. Experts are routinely hired by trial lawyers to help develop clothing strategies for attorneys, clients, and witnesses in a trial. These experts are attuned to the various clothing styles, colors, and fabrics that can convey different messages.

If, for example, you come into court wearing a bright red leather miniskirt and see-through blouse, you will project a provocative image. When you appear flashy in court, a male judge might view you as either provocative or cheap, and a female judge will simply view you as trashy. On the other hand, a dark dress with pearls, or a sedate beige dress with a floral print and collar, will convey a more conservative attitude.

Appearance is everything. If you present the wrong look to the judge, it could result in a significant reduction in your property settlement and alimony award.

## Dress Conservatively

While the following recommendations may seem sexist, the truth is that they will have an impact on your case. Unfortunately, the court is a place where not only legal judgments are passed. Judgments based on appearances are more subtly, though no less convincingly, rendered. If you appear sweet, demure, and feminine, a female or a male judge will be impressed by your conservatism.

In choosing the colors of your clothing, keep to soft colors or pastels. Nothing too bright should be worn, but especially avoid red. Try to wear as little black as possible, because it projects an image of strength. You don't want to appear too strong in court. Appearing weak and defenseless will do much to strengthen your position as the underdog—the less advantaged litigant in the divorce proceedings.

Wear knee-length dresses and avoid miniskirts or long skirts with a slit up the side or back. You want to conform to the image of the average woman, even though you are not. If you normally wear silk and linen and purchase your wardrobe at upscale department stores, you should not wear those types of clothes to court.

Judges are fooled routinely. One old lawyer maxim says that in all cases in court nationwide, about twenty percent of the witnesses lie. In criminal cases, about fifty percent of the witnesses lie. In divorce cases, eighty percent of the witnesses lie. There is a great amount of truth to this expression. Judges look with a skeptical eye at the demeanor of witnesses who may be lying for financial gain. The more conservative and credible you appear, the greater the chance the judge will view your testimony as truthful.

If you are claiming marital torts and abuse against your husband, your clothes should represent your lack of self-esteem. If you appear meek and banal, you will effectively convey an image of insecurity.

If you watched the Bobbitt case on national television, you heard the newscasters commenting on the style of clothing worn by both parties during the trial. Substantial thought was devoted to the attire of both parties so they would appear to be something other than they were.

Similarly, in the O.J. Simpson case, the prosecutor changed her hairstyle both before and during the trial at the recommendation of consultants who were attempting to soften her image before the jury.

Criminal defendants who normally wear orange prison garb are allowed to dress in street clothes when they appear before a jury. Allowing regular dress diminishes the preconceived notion that the person is guilty because they are awaiting trial behind bars.

This psychological notion is the same in all trials. First impressions are long-lasting and rarely change. Do not make the mistake of creating the wrong first impression. Impress the judge with your candor, credibility, and conservative nature by wearing the appropriate clothes.

*Strategy 42.* In court, dress conservatively and act in a conservative manner.

169

# Wear a Conservative Hairstyle, Jewelry, and Makeup

Hairstyle, jewelry, and makeup can say as much about your demeanor and credibility as clothing. If you usually wear your hair long and flowing, don't for your divorce hearing—this type of hairstyle will present a provocative image.

Many lawyers recommend that their female clients wear their hair conservatively. One of the most common hairstyles seen in conservative communities is a traditional blunt cut with the hair pulled back in a simple bow. Presenting the image of a conservative yuppie wife will always convey an air of tradition.

If you have curly or wavy hair, keep it pulled back with a bow or clasp. You do not want your hair flowing around your face and covering it up. The judge will look at your face, your eyes, your hair, and your overall appearance to arrive at a perception of you as a person. Months of planning can be destroyed at once if you do not make the effort to look genuinely conservative and credible as a witness and litigant.

Different makeup styles can also lead a judge to mentally place you in a particular stereotype. You do not want to be perceived as glamorous, provocative, or vexing. Think of how makeup can make one look. Take the extreme example of Tammy Faye Baker, with her long eyelashes, rouge, and heavy eye shadow. Obviously, a presentation such as hers can be damaging in the courtroom.

Makeup should be used sparingly, in earth tones and lighter shades. Do not wear red, bright pink, bright blue, or other dark, deep, or bright colors. You want to appear like a schoolmarm, not a movie star.

Jewelry can also project different images. Too much conveys an image of arrogance. Keep in mind that judges are not paid large salaries and may harbor hidden grudges toward wealthy or seemingly conceited people.

Wear only your wedding ring to court. Avoid flashy necklaces, earrings, or other bright, shiny objects. If you plead poverty in court and are attempting to get a large settlement, wearing elaborate or expensive jewelry will inevitably contradict your claims.

If you normally wear contact lenses, wear your glasses to court instead. Many lawyers do this. They know that law is very conservative, and to thrive within it, one must appear conservative.

If a male lawyer normally wears pinky rings outside of court, he might remove the jewelry. Some lawyers may even own an alternative wedding band without diamonds to wear to court.

# Testify Demurely

Although you can do everything in your power to appear sedate and conservative, your behavior in the courtroom will ultimately define you as a person. If you behave arrogantly, argumentatively, or obnoxiously, a judge will not develop a sympathetic attitude toward you. He or she will be less inclined to consider your best interests in the final outcome of the case.

During all of your legal proceedings, you should remain calm and level-headed, regardless of how exasperating a situation becomes. This may be extremely difficult, but continue to remind yourself that it will help you in the long run. If you can play the role of the demure and demoralized woman who has been victimized throughout her marriage, you will engage the court's sympathies and it will eventually reward you.

In the end, if you are able to present yourself as an ordinary wife who has been disadvantaged by the intentional and malicious acts of her husband, you will come out on top. Remember that nothing is certain—there are no guarantees in life—but if you follow the rules, you will increase your chances of winning your case.

# Chapter 18

# Strategies for Minimizing Tax Liability

One of the ultimate goals of any divorce lawyer is to protect his or her client from tax liability in a divorce settlement. This liability can arise from two often-overlooked areas: taxation and bankruptcy. Too often, a lawyer is not schooled in the tax considerations of the court's dissolution of the marital estate. Many malpractice claims against lawyers have occurred because of their ignorance of laws on taxation or bankruptcy. Protect yourself by hiring a lawyer who has training in tax law as well as domestic law.

In previous chapters, you have learned that child support payments are not taxable, while alimony payments are, and in many instances, the division of equity from your home may not be taxable as well. You and your lawyer must weigh all the consequences of receiving property distribution versus alimony to make the right decision.

The taxation of alimony is its only drawback—you may have to bite the bullet and pay the tax man. However, the following discussion should enable you to better understand some of the laws concerning bankruptcy and taxation so that you will be wary of their potential pitfalls.

If your husband files for bankruptcy, U.S. bankruptcy laws will not allow him to avoid alimony and child support. However, he can avoid property settlement orders or orders that require him to pay other debts of the marriage. In fact, he can discharge every other order of the court to his heart's desire.

A savvy, spiteful husband will attempt to structure his divorce settlement to avoid child support and alimony, and then declare bankruptcy to avoid debts on other assets. Beware—your husband could convince you to take increased property on which he pays the continuing debt after the divorce, rather than provide you with increased child support and alimony to enable you to pay the debt.

Some recent cases may be changing this in various areas of the country. You should certainly study the possibility of a bankruptcy filing by your husband after the divorce.

For example, if you are awarded the marital residence, your husband may cleverly trick you into agreeing that he will assume the house payments rather than pay you alimony to cover the house payments. Assuming he is not too wealthy to eliminate bankruptcy as an option, he can file a Chapter Seven bankruptcy that will terminate his obligation to pay your house payments forever. In that case, you will lose the house.

To safeguard against this, you should ask for alimony and child support to cover the house payments so that you can assume the indebtedness and control the future of your property ownership.

However, if your husband is so rich that he cannot file for bankruptcy without the risk of losing his remaining assets, you need not follow this advice.

---

***Strategy 43.*** *Be certain to consult with your lawyer about the effect of your husband's filing for bankruptcy after your divorce as it relates to your division of the marital estate.*

---

Because of your husband's ability to file for bankruptcy after the divorce, you must have counseling from your lawyer and accountant to know how best to structure any agreed property distribution and award of child support and alimony. Divorce lawyers tend to forget about the power of a bankruptcy case. Many lawyers know little about tax laws, and even less about bankruptcy laws. Whenever you assume the debt on property you keep after the divorce, request alimony and child support to help cover the indebtedness so the debt can't be wiped out in bankruptcy.

Always insist on alimony unless you are planning on a quick remarriage or living with your lover. Alimony will usually terminate when you remarry or live with a man. In either event, you should consult with your lawyer about property distribution and child support, which are not necessarily tied to either of these two events.

---

*Strategy 44.* *Assume long-term debt obligations—if the court awards alimony to cover the debt, and if you are allowed to retain the property.*

---

In many instances the marital residence will not be kept by either spouse. The court will order it to be sold and the equity split. Of course, there are many reasons why the court might award the marital residence to one spouse over the other. Look for these reasons with your lawyer. One of the most common reasons is the desire of the court system to allow the minor children of a marriage to continue residing in the marital residence until they reach eighteen years of age. This prevents the children from upheaval and additional emotional trauma. Courts are sympathetic to the best interests of the children of a marriage. Another valid reason might be the health and medical condition of one spouse. Where there is little or no equity in the home to divide, courts will consider allowing one party to retain the residence and continue with the obligation of the mortgage payments.

To determine whether debts against property should be assumed by you or your husband, you will need to carefully consider several factors. There is no general rule that tells you how to get your husband to pay the debt without risking wiping it out in bankruptcy. But structuring your divorce settlement properly ensures that your husband will continue paying the debt.

The following are factors you should consider in determining whether to assume a long-term debt.

1.  Will the court allow you to keep the property that has the debt attached to it? (e.g., car, home, boat, vacation home). If you are going to sell the property, you certainly do not want the debt, but if the court will allow you to keep the property, you want alimony to pay it.

2.  How wealthy is your husband? Is he so wealthy that he has too many assets to lose by filing bankruptcy? If so, you have nothing to worry about if he assumes the debt. On the other hand, if he is just moderately wealthy or typically middle-class, he will stand a far better chance of filing bankruptcy.

    If he owns his own business, it is possible that he may fraudulently transfer all his assets into another entity or person's name to avoid paying the divorce settlement. Ask your lawyer or accountant to evaluate your husband's potential for filing bankruptcy after the divorce is final.

3.  Do you really want a particular asset, or can you live with selling it and receiving your share of the proceeds? If the property has sentimental value to you,

then you might consider keeping it. Or perhaps your husband wants a particular asset more than any other item. His desire for it may be reason enough to keep him from acquiring it. Vengeance can be a goal in and of itself, so you may feel compelled to pursue ownership of the property. However, don't let vengeance override logical decision making when determining what property to keep.

4. Is the debt on the item small enough that it will not be overly burdensome for you to pay it? Should you retain the property if he fails to pay or if he chooses to file bankruptcy? Never bite off more than you can chew.

5. Can the debt be paid out of child support or alimony? Don't take the property unless you can pay for it with income that your husband gives you by court order.

Don't forget Strategy 44, which cautioned you to assume long-term debts if you receive alimony to cover the obligation. The five factors stated previously point out varying reasons to carefully analyze any decision to assume long-term debt. Only do so when it benefits you and causes detriment to your husband. Study the equities carefully, and speak to your lawyer and your accountant before making the final decision. You may want to take on long-term obligations that are paid for by alimony guaranteed for a term equivalent to the length of time payments will be owed on the property, if the property has sentimental value to you, or in some other way is important to you.

## Term Cash Payments as Property Distribution

You and your lawyer must be certain to have the court order show that any cash payments are for distribution of property owned prior to the divorce. This will eliminate taxation of the cash payments to you. It applies to payments your husband has made out of his pocket by cash, check, or other monetary instrument either prior to the divorce decree or at any time after your final divorce is awarded.

Husbands love to give money to wives and tell them it is for purchasing groceries or other necessary items. When it comes time to collect the money your husband owes you for child support or alimony, you can be sure he will claim the money was given to you for temporary or permanent child support or alimony. He certainly did not give it to you out of the goodness of his heart. When your husband can show the money is for payment of alimony, he will receive a deduction on his own taxes, and you will then have to pay taxes on the money you received. The only way to avoid this is to classify all cash payments as property distribution in the court order of your divorce.

There are other ways in which a payment can be considered to be nondeductible or nonincludible as alimony. You and your husband may elect out of alimony treatment for support payments by making a provision in your property settlement agreement that certain payments are not meant to constitute alimony for tax purposes. Your lawyer should be able to include or exclude the appropriate language which will benefit you most if he can obtain the agreement of your husband's lawyer.

---

*Strategy 45.* *Always keep a log of cash payments made to you by your husband, including the reasons the payments were made.*

---

If you still receive cash payments and cannot classify them in a court order as property distribution, keep a written diary or log of the times, dates, amounts, and reasons for receiving the money. Every time your husband gives you two hundred dollars, write it down to prove it was for property distribution of marital assets or child support help, so that it is not taxable to you.

# Clearly Describe Alimony/Property Distribution

Lawyers do not always follow the proper laws in creating a property settlement agreement for your final divorce. In fact, a commonly claimed malpractice suit against lawyers arises from the drafting of property settlement agreements, and from the lawyer's failure to designate an item properly as alimony or a property distribution.

You certainly do not want to pay taxes on money distributed to you if you can possibly avoid it. Why give your husband the benefit of a tax deduction if it isn't necessary? Only skilled legal and accounting experts can help to determine the appropriate way to draft the agreement.

If your settlement agreement is poorly worded, you might have to pay taxes when you really shouldn't. Classifying the award to you as a property distribution will help to alleviate the tax burden of the divorce.

Your first consideration before you sign a property settlement agreement should be whether or not you will be taxed as a result of signing the legal document. By analyzing the tax structure of your divorce award, you protect yourself after divorce. Thousands of cases exist in which a husband's divorce lawyer structured a divorce settlement for a tax benefit for his client, and the wife's unskilled lawyer recommended that she sign the agreement without ever considering the effect it had on her. You should always investigate the proposed settlement with your accountant as well as your lawyer, so that all consequences can be logically evaluated.

*Strategy 46. Structure your divorce settlement to minimize tax liability.*

# Chapter 19 | *Avoid the Pitfalls of Alimony Clauses*

Thousands of women have been tricked into agreeing to alimony that is contingent upon three clauses most commonly used to terminate the husband's obligation to pay. Those three contingencies are normally stated as follows:

1. Alimony terminates in the event of the death of the wife.
2. Alimony terminates in the event of remarriage of the wife.
3. Alimony terminates in the event of cohabitation of the wife with a member of the opposite sex who is not related to her.

Courts have developed other contingencies to terminate alimony, but these three are the ones most frequently used. Contingency number one, your death, is the one contingency not worth fighting over. You can't take your alimony with you.

Remember, nothing is written in stone, and you do not have to agree to these contingencies. When you agree to a property settlement including alimony, the courts will usually accept that agreement and make it part of the divorce, as long as it contains some degree of fairness. Smart husbands will insist upon all three contingencies, but savvy wives will agree to none. At best, you can hope to compromise.

You may not be given the opportunity to agree or to choose a contingency. If you and your husband can't come to terms, the court will make the alimony decision, and the judge will decide which contingent events will terminate your alimony. If this happens, you will be given the three contingencies stated above.

Another case history will be helpful in understanding how alimony clauses can have a disastrous effect on your emotional and financial well-being.

> Marie had been married to her husband for thirty-two years. During the marriage, she and her husband had amassed a fortune in real estate holdings, most of which was connected to her husband's business. Because of this connection, Marie did not want to take the real estate holdings.
>
> Against the advice of her counsel, she sought alimony. In the state where she resided, there was a law saying that alimony terminated at ten years unless the parties agreed to continue payment past that point. Marie's husband was not ignorant; he adamantly refused to pay any alimony past ten years. He insisted that the alimony award be contingent upon her death, remarriage, or cohabitation with a member of the opposite sex. He received three and a half million dollars in real estate holdings, and agreed to pay her the tidy sum of fifteen thousand dollars a month for ten years. This appeared to be worth one million eight hundred thousand dollars over the ten years, or more than half the value of the real estate. But Marie did not take into consideration the federal and state tax laws, which took almost forty percent of the amount in taxes and reduced the total alimony receipt to only one million and eighty thousand dollars—a drop of seven hundred twenty thousand dollars.
>
> Two years after the divorce, Marie became lonely and began living with a new male friend. Her husband hired a detective to prove she was cohabiting with a member of the opposite sex. The divorce court terminated her alimony award after she had received only twenty-six months of alimony.

> Over the twenty-six months she received nine thousand dollars a month after taxes. Overall, she had received only $234,000 after paying taxes. Her husband walked away with over three million dollars in real estate holdings and was allowed to deduct all of the payments of alimony from his income tax liability.

This is an extreme example of how badly you can get cheated in your divorce. Perhaps you will want new male companionship after the divorce has taken place. You will need to guard yourself from the tax man by getting the advice of skilled professionals when you decide to choose alimony or property distribution. Placing contingencies on your ability to receive your fair share of the marital estate creates benefits to your husband that may prove disastrous to you later on. Sometimes it is better to obtain property distribution rather than taxable alimony payments. Be aware of the tax implications of any settlement you enter into.

# Limit the Number of Clauses

You should convince your husband to agree to an alimony settlement agreement in which death is the only contingency. But if he insists on either the remarriage or the cohabitation clause, you should choose the remarriage clause. You can always live with your new lover while your ex-husband provides you with a healthy monthly stipend to pay for your home, vacations, dinners out, and various other necessities of life.

When negotiating with your husband in the conference room, spring your tape-recorded evidence on him. Use this weapon to convince him to give up as many of these contingencies as possible. Get him to agree to the longest possible period of alimony. If you are in a state that allows alimony for life, ask for it.

---

*Strategy 47.* *When seeking alimony in a property settlement agreement, contractually agree with your husband to minimize the contingent events that may terminate your right to alimony.*

---

## Avoid the Appearance of Cohabitation

If you simply must live with your new lover, you should avoid the appearance of cohabiting with him. Do your neighbors know you are living together? Once they do, your ex-husband, and certainly his detective, will know about it, too.

Your alimony payments are your means of survival in the postdivorce period. Perhaps your new lover wants to spend every waking moment next to you. Perhaps you want to be able to wake up in the morning to make love in your own comfortable house. But your ex-husband will have a completely different idea and plan.

He will hire a detective to prevent you from receiving the money you are entitled to. Photographs will show your lover's car at your house at six in the morning and will prove he is there at eleven at night. Your ex's detective will testify in court and provide a series of photos with times and dates on them to establish that your lover is with you every day at these times for a solid month. Even to the casual observer, it will appear that you are cohabiting with a man.

Worse yet, once your former husband finds evidence that you are not living alone with his children, he will be able to file a motion to change child custody and support. Many courts allow a motion to change custody whenever there is a material change in circumstances or when it is in the best interests of the minor children.

## Avoid the Pitfalls of Alimony Clauses

You can bet the judge won't think your living with another man out of wedlock is in the best interests of the minor children. You may end up losing custody of your children. It will then be you who is paying the child support.

In this postdivorce period, it is extremely important to hide cohabitation with your lover from your ex-spouse. Motions are routinely filed to terminate alimony when an ex-husband and his detective prove or think they have proven cohabitation. The clause in your divorce decree means just what it states—you lose your alimony when your husband proves you are cohabiting with a man.

How can you protect yourself against losing alimony when you are cohabiting with a member of the opposite sex? Possibly the easiest way to protect yourself is to negotiate a property settlement agreement containing alimony without this contingency. However, in the likely event that you are unable to convince your husband and his wily attorney to agree to omit this contingency clause, you will have only one avenue to pursue.

Disguise and concealment are your only options. If you must live with your lover, take all of the following steps. They may not prevent you from losing your alimony, but they will certainly decrease your chances.

1. Watch out for detectives. Videotape is a powerful tool. If you notice an unknown vehicle routinely parked near your residence or place of work, be careful! By being aware of your surroundings, you can help to avoid being photographed and videotaped.

2. When your lover lives with you, make sure his car is always in the garage. If there is no garage, keep his car hidden several blocks away. Have him observe the area outside the house before leaving. Detectives becomes bored quickly. If they don't see the necessary evidence, they will make routine stops by your resi-

dence rather than constantly sitting outside hoping for a photograph. Keep your car hidden as well.

3.  Change your normal habits and customs. If you eat at a certain place every Wednesday with your lover, change the location, time, and day each week. Do you work out at a particular gym with him or travel with him to routine leisure spots? Change all of the usual places where you can be seen and photographed. A detective will become frustrated when he is unable to establish a pattern of habit and will be less able to establish necessary evidence. Do you come home at a quarter after five and meet your lover every day after work? Change this time so it is harder to track.

4.  Keep your window shades drawn to avoid photographic evidence that your lover is inside the house with you. When the detective can't see you, he can't photograph your lover.

5.  Avoid having any utility bills or other bills sent in your lover's name to your residence. Do not have any bills with both of your names. Avoid joint checking and savings accounts. Evidence of this type will quickly convince a judge you are cohabiting with your lover.

6.  Do not let mail come to your residence in your lover's name. Have him acquire a post office box. Better yet, have him use a friend's residence to receive mail. Evidence of this type can be used to disprove the cohabitation.

7.  Do not tell any of your neighbors that your lover lives with you. Witnesses in court can be as convincing as photographs. For example, if your nosy neighbors testify that they see your lover pick up the morning paper every day or routinely see him arriving home after five P.M., their observations will be damaging to you.

Do whatever it takes to prove that your lover does not live with you, or that you do not live with him. Your income and future depend upon it.

*Strategy 48.* *To protect your alimony, child custody, and child support, you should avoid cohabiting with a member of the opposite sex.*

# Chapter 20 | *Plan for Your Future*

Certainly, many of you will be overwhelmed with grief at the prospect of obtaining a divorce. It will undoubtedly be one of the most difficult things that you will ever go through. Nevertheless, you must remember that you owe it to yourself to get the most out of your divorce. The advice in this book may seem somewhat unscrupulous. Yet it is based on the experiences of lawyers and women over many years. It is intended to empower you and help you get what you deserve.

When a businessman is starting up a new business or approaching a venture capitalist for a loan, the single most important tool for his success is his business plan. The business plan for the future growth of the company is the logical, preconceived blueprint for success.

Preserving your assets and alimony to maximize your ability to recover from your divorce is analogous to the business plan. It must also be a rational, logical, well-thought-out strategy, designed with the single purpose of winning. It must establish a step-by-step plan of attack.

You have set goals for yourself throughout your life. Remember when you decided to learn to play the piano, train your singing voice, or excel in athletics? Do you remember setting the goal to graduate from college or professional school?

Now is the time to set out and realize one more goal in your life—freedom.

Possible goals might include some of the following:

1. To establish independence from your husband.
2. To establish financial independence.
3. To find someone who will appreciate your love.
4. To end your servitude to an ungrateful husband.
5. To find happiness in life.
6. To better your status in life.
7. To preserve your mental and emotional well-being.
8. To eliminate abuse from your life.
9. To find a partner and soul mate.
10. To find a best friend to share your life with.
11. To be successful.
12. To get an education comparable to your husband's or better.

No matter what your goal is, store it mentally where it cannot be located by your husband, and define a step-by-step plan to achieve it.

Whenever your goal requires financial support, you must find out how much it will cost to obtain it. If your goal is to get an education, meet with a counselor at a local college to determine how long you'll need to spend in school and exactly how much it will cost.

Will your salary allow you to live independently without the assistance of your husband, or do you need financial support from alimony or child support? A household with two incomes has more disposable income than a household with only one. Unless you make more than your husband, the obvious answer is that you will need financial support to reach your goals.

If abuse is a major concern that frightens you and impairs your ability to leave, you will need the aid of an expert such as a lawyer. The law provides women relief from spousal abuse. Planning for this relief will create additional obstacles, but counseling will help you determine the appropriate steps to take.

Financial independence may be one of your chosen goals. Planning to get half of every dime you and your husband own will take thorough, methodical planning and investigation. Once you determine your husband's approximate net worth, you will need legal advice to obtain the proper judicial relief that will award you half of the assets. When you receive these assets, make sure you conserve, save, and use them wisely, as this will help protect your financial future.

No matter what goal you seek, plan for the goal by determining how you can best reach it. Planning for your future is a task which deserves lengthy consideration and thought. Once the divorce is over, it's too late to change your situation.

When all is said and done, you don't have to be the loser in a divorce. By thoroughly planning your strategy, you can be the winner. Don't look back. Look forward to fun—and to the pursuit of happiness, which the Declaration of Independence claims is your inalienable right.

Now, with your knowledge of the intricacies of the judicial and government systems, you can control your own destiny. You can to create and implement a strategic plan for your divorce war. You do not have to stay poor, unhappily married, or trapped in an abusive relationship. With a strategic divorce plan, the right lawyer, and a little luck, you can change your life.

Most people accept the status quo and avoid change. But you don't have to be like everyone else. Where is it written that you must follow the rules set by society? Who cares what the majority wants? Isn't it better to experience all of life's wonders than to accept a safe, secure, but unhappy life? No one else can live your life for you. If you decide that a divorce is the only way to change and improve your life, you have the knowledge to go after it successfully.

*Strategy 49. When preparing your plan for divorce, be certain that you have properly determined all goals you desire to reach.*

# Chapter 21 | *Avenues to Pursue Once the Divorce Is Final*

Of course you hope that you will be the winner in your divorce. Unfortunately, however, one person in a divorce situation must necessarily lose. If you happen to be that person, there are several procedures by which you can attempt to legally change the judicial decision.

The most common legal procedure used to alter the judicial award is a Motion for New Trial. This is a legal motion, usually filed within a few days to a couple of weeks following the trial. Its purpose is to request a modification of the award and order of the court. In most states there will be a statute informing your legal counsel of the factors permitted for bringing such a motion.

Motions of this type are routinely filed at the close of a divorce but are rarely successful. Typically, most judges will not reverse their decisions without overwhelming evidence to support such a reversal. Here are some of the most common reasons for allowing a new trial:

1.  Your motion establishes in the judge's mind that he has committed a legal error by failing to follow a statute or case precedent.
2.  Your attorney is able to produce new evidence that was not considered in the original trial.

3. You are able to produce proof that some of the evidence in your original trial was fraudulent or had been fraudulently concealed from the judge.

A second, less frequently used procedure for reversing your divorce is an appeal. An appeal is a legal proceeding brought after the conclusion of a case to challenge factual findings of the court or legal interpretations made by the court. Appeals are brought from the lower court where your divorce was heard to a higher court in the state, which reviews decisions of the lower courts.

Most appeals will not disturb the factual finding of the divorce judge unless there are some highly unusual circumstances. Suffice it to say that it is a rare day when an appeals court will reevaluate the facts of a case. However, it is done on occasion. When an appeals court believes that a lower court decision is so egregious that no reasonable person or fact-finder would have ruled in the same manner as the court, the appeals court will step in to evaluate the facts. Most of the time, however, appeals courts simply leave the fact-finding to the discretion of the judge unless an abuse of discretion can be shown. An abuse of discretion is almost never found by an appeals court.

The reasoning of an appeals court is that the judge hearing the evidence is in the best position to determine the credibility of the parties and witnesses. When an appeal is undertaken, the parties involved in the divorce do not have a new trial at the appeals court level. The higher court reviews evidence in the original case along with legal arguments of the lawyers involved. If an appeal is successful, the possible results include a new trial, a reversal of the judge's ruling, or some other appropriate legal relief deemed appropriate by the court. For example, if the circumstances warranted increasing an award of alimony, the higher court could remand the case to the original divorce court with instructions to the judge to make a new determination on the amount and term of alimony for the wife.

However, there are substantial problems with bringing an appeal in your divorce. They are usually expensive, are time-consuming, and are rarely successful. Appellate courts tend to go out of their way to leave the status quo intact, failing to reverse the lower-court decisions in the majority of cases.

This does not mean that you should not consider an appeal in an unfruitful divorce case, as every case turns upon its own individual circumstances. No general rule exists to determine which type of cases can be successfully or unsuccessfully appealed. The ultimate point is that you should think very carefully before you decide to make an appeal. Your lawyer will have a financial stake in continuing the litigation after your divorce has been lost. If he charges you by the hour for his services, he may not have your best interests at heart.

While legal appeals are rarely successful, motions to modify child custody, child support, or alimony have a much greater success rate. Each state will have different rules to follow when filing a motion to modify child custody, child support, or alimony.

Some states have prohibitions on filing motions in alimony situations. To protect yourself, you should have your lawyer attempt to include a legal clause in the final divorce decree that allows you to bring a motion for additional support if your circumstances change. The disadvantage to this type of clause is that your husband will also have the right to modify his payments in the event that his circumstances change.

Child custody and support are issues frequently litigated following a divorce. A change in circumstances of one of the parents or the minor children is frequently used as a basis for attempting to change the divorce order. When your income decreases or your ex-husband's income increases, your ability to change the court order is an advantage. However, many other factors exist that will allow you to make various modifi-cations—your lawyer will be able to determine the appropriate legal procedure to help you reach your goals.

Remember, there are legal procedures that you can utilize in the event that you lose your divorce. It is up to you to con-tinue the battle if you feel you have been unfairly treated by the court.

---

*Strategy 50.* *You need to go all out to win your divorce the first time, because appeals are rarely won.*

---

# Appendix A | *Laws*

## Caveat 1

The information on marital tort suits in the following table does not include all categories of marital tort suits. This column of the table concerns the abolishment of the spousal immunity doctrine. The abolishment of this doctrine allows spouses to sue each other under certain limited circumstances. A "yes" in this column does not mean that all forms of tort suits against spouses are allowed. Each state varies, with substantial difference in the type of marital tort suits that are allowed. Many of the states with a "yes" designation have only partially abrogated the doctrine, allowing motor vehicle accident claims of one spouse against another. The laws are changing rapidly. It is imperative that you seek legal advice from a local attorney to learn the type of tort suits allowed in your state.

## Caveat 2

"Equitable/M" indicates the state follows marital distribution laws that are similar to, but not synonymous with, those in equitable distribution states.

197

### Caveat 3

"Community/mod" indicates the state follows community property principles with a slight modification, usually leaning towards equitable distribution.

| | Marital Tort Suits Allowed? | Fault or No-Fault Grounds | Property Distribution | Statutes on Alimony? |
|---|---|---|---|---|
| Alabama | Yes | Both | Equitable | Yes |
| Alaska | Yes | Both | Equitable | Yes |
| Arizona | Yes | No-Fault | Community | Yes |
| Arkansas | Yes | Fault | Community/mod | Yes |
| California | Yes | No-Fault | Community | Yes |
| Colorado | Yes | No-Fault | Equitable | Yes |
| Connecticut | Yes | Both | Equitable | Yes |
| Delaware | Yes | Both | Equitable | Yes |
| District of Columbia | Yes | No-Fault | Equitable | Yes |
| Florida | No | Both | Equitable | Yes |
| Georgia | Yes | Both | Equitable | Yes |
| Hawaii | No | No-Fault | Equitable | Yes |
| Idaho | Yes | Both | Equitable | Yes |
| Illinois | Yes | Both | Equitable/M | Yes |
| Indiana | Yes | No-Fault | Equitable | Yes |
| Iowa | Yes | No-Fault | Equitable | Yes |
| Kansas | Yes | No-Fault | Equitable | Yes |
| Kentucky | Yes | No-Fault | Equitable | Yes |
| Louisiana | Yes | No-Fault | Community/mod | Yes |
| Maine | Yes | Both | Equitable/M | Yes |
| Maryland | Yes | Fault | Equitable | Yes |
| Massachusetts | Yes | Both | Equitable | Yes |
| Michigan | Yes | No-Fault | Equitable | Yes |
| Minnesota | Yes | No-Fault | Equitable | Yes |
| Mississippi | Yes | Both | Equitable/M | Yes |
| Missouri | Yes | No-Fault | Equitable | Yes |
| Montana | Yes | No-Fault | Equitable | Yes |
| Nebraska | Yes | No-Fault | Equitable/M | Yes |
| Nevada | Yes | No-Fault | Community/mod | Yes |
| New Hampshire | Yes | Both | Equitable | Yes |
| New Jersey | Yes | Fault | Equitable | Yes |

# Laws

| | | | | |
|---|---|---|---|---|
| New Mexico | Yes | Both | Community | Yes |
| New York | Yes | Fault | Equitable | Yes |
| North Carolina | Yes | Fault | Equitable | Yes |
| North Dakota | Yes | Both | Equitable | Yes |
| Ohio | Yes | Both | Equitable/M | Yes |
| Oklahoma | Yes | Fault | Equitable | Yes |
| Oregon | Yes | Both | Equitable/M | Yes |
| Pennsylvania | Yes | Both | Equitable | Yes |
| Rhode Island | Yes | Both | Equitable | Yes |
| South Carolina | Yes | Fault | Equitable | Yes |
| South Dakota | Yes | Both | Equitable | Yes |
| Tennessee | Yes | Both | Equitable/M | Yes |
| Texas | Yes | Both | Equitable | Yes |
| Utah | Yes | Both | Equitable | Yes |
| Vermont | Yes | Both | Equitable | Yes |
| Virginia | Yes | Fault | Equitable | Yes |
| Washington | Yes | No-Fault | Equitable | Yes |
| West Virginia | Yes | Both | Equitable | Yes |
| Wisconsin | Yes | No-Fault | Equitable/M | Yes |
| Wyoming | Yes | No-Fault | Equitable | Yes |

## Appendix B | *Bar Associations*

The following listings provide addresses and telephone numbers of state bar associations and women's bar associations.

Alabama State Bar
P.O. Box 671
Montgomery, Alabama 36101
334-269-1515

Mobile Bar Association, Women Lawyers Section
P.O. Drawer 2005
Mobile, Alabama 36652
334-433-9790

Alaska Bar Association
P.O. Box 100279
Anchorage, Alaska 99510
907-272-7469

Anchorage Association of Women Lawyers
Box 550
W. 7th Avenue, Suite 1100
Anchorage, Alaska 99501
907-263-8255

State Bar of Arizona
111 W. Monroe, Suite 1800
Phoenix, Arizona 85003-1742
602-252-4804

Arizona Women Lawyers Association
c/o Susan Villarreal, President
44 E. Broadway
Tucson, Arizona 85701
520-620-7112

Arkansas Bar Association
400 West Markham
Little Rock, Arkansas 72201
501-375-4606

Arkansas Association of Women Lawyers
c/o Ann Orsi Smith, President
217 West 2nd Street, Suite 110
Little Rock, Arkansas 72201
501-374-0033

State Bar of California
555 Franklin Street
San Francisco, California 94102
415-561-8200

California Women Lawyers
926 J Street, Suite 905
Sacramento, California 95814
916-441-3703

# Bar Associations

Colorado Bar Association
1900 Grant Street, #950
Denver, Colorado 80203-4309
303-860-1112

Colorado Women's Bar Association
1801 Broadway #400
Denver, Colorado 80202
303-298-1313

Connecticut Bar Association
101 Corporate Place
Rocky Hill, Connecticut 06067
203-721-0025

Connecticut Bar Association
Women and the Law Section
101 Corporate Place
Rocky Hill, Connecticut 06067
203-721-0025

Delaware Bar Association
1201 Orange Street, Suite 1100
Wilmington, Delaware 19801
302-658-5279

Delaware State Bar Association
Section on Women and the Law
c/o Patricia Bartley Schwartz, President
222 Delaware Avenue, Suite 1220
Wilmington, Delaware 19801
302-594-4500

Women's Bar Association of DC
2000 L Street, NW, Suite 510
Washington, D.C. 20036
202-785-1540

Bar Association of the District of Columbia
1250 H Street, 6th floor
Washington, D.C. 20005
202-737-4700

The Florida Bar
The Florida Bar Center, 650 Apalachee Parkway
Tallahassee, Florida 32399
904-561-5600

Florida Association for Women Lawyers
c/o Elizabeth Ann Morgan, President
44 W. Flagler Street, Suite 1700
Miami, Florida 33130
305-530-0080

State Bar of Georgia
800 The Hurt Building
50 Hurt Plaza
Atlanta, Georgia 30303
404-527-8700

Georgia Association for Women Lawyers
c/o Roman White, President
68 Mitchell Street, Suite 4100
Atlanta, Georgia 30335-0332
404-330-6400

# Bar Associations

Hawaii State Bar Association
1136 Union Mall
Penthouse One
Honolulu, Hawaii 96813
808-537-1868

Hawaii Women Lawyers
c/o Pamela Byrne, Officer
300 Ale Moana Boulevard, Suite 7102
Honolulu, Hawaii 96813
808-541-2521

Idaho State Bar
P.O. Box 895
Boise, Idaho 83701-0895
208-334-4500

Idaho Women Lawyers, Inc.
c/o Judy Holcomb, President
P.O. Box 2720
Boise, Idaho 83701
208-342-6571

Illinois State Bar Association
Illinois Bar Center
424 S. 2nd Street
Springfield, Illinois 62701
217-525-1760

Women's Bar Association of Illinois
321 S. Plymouth Court, Suite 4S
Chicago, Illinois 60604
312-341-8530

Indiana State Bar Association
230 East Ohio Street, 4th floor
Indianapolis, Indiana 46204
317-639-5465

Indianapolis Bar Association, Women Lawyers Division
c/o Mary Ann Tippitt, President
10 North Senate Avenue
Indianapolis, Indiana 46204-2277
317-232-3268

Iowa State Bar Association
521 E. Locust, Suite 300
Des Moines, Iowa 50309-1939
515-243-3179

Iowa Organization of Women Attorneys
c/o Donna Sorenson, President
222 2nd Avenue SE
Cedar Rapids, Iowa 52420
319-368-4444

Kansas Bar Association
P.O. Box 1037
1200 Harrison Street
Topeka, Kansas 66601
913-234-5696

Wichita Women Lawyers, Wichita Bar Association
700 Epic Center, 301 North Main
Wichita, Kansas 67202
316-263-2251

# Bar Associations

Kentucky Bar Association
514 West Main
Frankfort, Kentucky 40601-1883
502-564-3795

Kentucky Bar Association for Women
c/o Ruth Baxter, President
P.O. Box 70212
Louisville, Kentucky 40270-0212
502-732-6688

Louisiana State Bar Association
601 Saint Charles Avenue
New Orleans, Louisiana 70130
504-566-1600

Louisiana Association for Women Attorneys
c/o Paula George, President
228 Saint Charles Avenue, Suite 207
New Orleans, Louisiana 70130
504-525-8832

Maine State Bar Association
124 State Street, P.O. Box 788
Augusta, Maine 04332-0788
207-622-7523

Maine State Bar Association, Women Lawyers Section
c/o Emily Bloch
P.O. Box 4510
Portland, Maine 04112
207-775-7271

Maryland State Bar Association, Inc.
520 West Fayette Street
Baltimore, Maryland 21201
410-685-7878

Women's Bar Association of Maryland
WBA-MD State Bar Center
520 West Fayette Street
Baltimore, Maryland 21201
410-528-9681

Massachusetts Bar Association
20 West Street
Boston, Massachusetts 02111-1218
617-542-3602

Women's Bar Association of Massachusetts
101 Tremont Street, Suite 611
Boston, Massachusetts 02108
617-695-1851

Minnesota State Bar Association
514 Nicollet Mall, Suite 300
Minneapolis, Minnesota 55402
612-333-1183

Minnesota Women Lawyers, Inc.
514 Nicollet Mall, Suite 350B
Minneapolis, Minnesota 55402
612-338-3205

Mississippi State Bar
P.O. Box 2168
Jackson, Mississippi 39225
601-948-4471

# Bar Associations

Mississippi Women Lawyers Association
P.O. Box 862
Jackson, Mississippi 39205-0862

The Missouri Bar
P.O. Box 119
Jefferson City, Missouri 65102
314-635-4128

Association of Women Lawyers of Greater Kansas City
c/o Chris Sill-Rogers, President
P.O. Box 419251
Kansas City, Missouri 64141

State Bar of Montana
46 N. Last Chance Gulch, Suite 2A
P.O. Box 577
Helena, Montana 59624
406-442-7660

State Bar of Montana, Women's Law Section
P.O. Box 577
Helena, Montana 59624
406-442-7660

Nebraska State Bar Association
635 South 14th Street
P.O. Box 81809
Lincoln, Nebraska 68508-1809
402-475-7091

Nebraska State Bar Association, Women and the Law Section
c/o Roberta L. Christensen, Chairperson
1125 S. 103rd Street, #800
Omaha, Nebraska 68127
402-390-9500

State Bar of Nevada
295 Holcomb Avenue, Suite 2
Reno, Nevada 89502-1085
702-329-4100

Northern Nevada Women Lawyers Association
Capitol Building
Carson City, Nevada 89710
702-687-5670

New Hampshire Bar Association
12 Pleasant Street
Concord, New Hampshire 03301
603-224-6942

New Jersey State Bar Association
1 Constitution Square
New Brunswick, New Jersey 08901
908-249-5000

New Jersey Women Lawyers Association
c/o New Jersey State Bar Association
1 Constitution Square
New Brunswick, New Jersey 08901
908-249-5000

State Bar of New Mexico
P.O. Box 25883
Albuquerque, New Mexico 87125
505-842-6132

New Mexico Women's Bar Association
P.O. Drawer 887
Albuquerque, New Mexico 87103
505-842-8255

# Bar Associations

New York State Bar Association
One Elk Street
Albany, New York 12207
518-463-3200

Women's Bar Association of the State of New York
c/o Barbara Odwak, Officer
32 Court Street, Suite 804
Brooklyn, New York 11201
718-875-1611

North Carolina State Bar
P.O. Box 25908
Raleigh, North Carolina 27611
919-828-4620

North Carolina Association of Women Attorneys
P.O. Box 1593
Durham, North Carolina 27702
919-479-2032

North Carolina Bar Association
P.O. Box 3688
Cary, North Carolina 27519
919-677-0561

State Bar Association of North Dakota
P.O. Box 2136
Bismarck, North Dakota 58502
701-255-1404

State Bar Association of North Dakota, Women Lawyers Section
c/o Connie Triplett, Chairperson
P.O. Box 5178
Grand Forks, North Dakota 58206
701-746-8488

Ohio State Bar Association
1700 Lakeshore Drive
Columbus, Ohio 43204
614-487-2050

Women in the Profession
c/o Barbara Howard, Chairperson
120 E. 4th Street, Suite 1200
Cincinnati, Ohio 45202
513-421-7300

Oklahoma Bar Association
P.O. Box 53036
Oklahoma City, Oklahoma 73152
405-524-2365

Women Lawyers in Oklahoma
c/o Debra Bruce
Oklahoma Bar Association
P.O. Box 53036
Oklahoma City, Oklahoma 73152
405-524-2365

Oregon State Bar
5200 SW Meadows Road
P.O. Box 1689
Lake Oswego, Oregon 97035
503-620-0222

Oregon Women Lawyers
P.O. Box 40393
Portland, Oregon 97240
503-221-2135

# Bar Associations

Pennsylvania Bar Association
100 South Street
P.O. Box 186
Harrisburg, Pennsylvania 17108
717-238-6715

Women's Law Project
125 S. 9th Street
Philadelphia, Pennsylvania 19103
215-928-9801

Puerto Rico Bar Association
Apartados 1900
San Juan, Puerto Rico 00903
809-721-3358

Rhode Island Bar Association
115 Cedar Street
Providence, Rhode Island 02903
401-421-5740

Rhode Island Women's Bar Association
c/o Denise Myers, President
Asquith, Mohoney, and Robinson
Providence, Rhode Island 02903
401-331-9100

South Carolina Bar
P.O. Box 608
Columbia, South Carolina 29202-0608
803-799-6653

South Carolina Women Lawyers Association
c/o Dara Cothran, President
P.O. Box 12399
Columbia, South Carolina 29211
803-799-9772

State Bar of South Dakota
222 East Capitol
Pierre, South Dakota 57501
605-224-7554

Tennessee Bar Association
3622 West End Avenue
Nashville, Tennessee 37205
615-383-7421

Tennessee Lawyer's Association for Women
249 Westfield Drive
Nashville, Tennessee 37221
615-646-2954

State Bar of Texas
P.O. Box 12487
Austin, Texas 78711-2487
512-475-1463

State Bar Association of Texas, Women and the Law
500 E. San Antonio, Room 602
El Paso, Texas 79901
915-546-2141

Utah State Bar
645 South, 200 East
Salt Lake City, Utah 84111
801-531-9077

# Bar Associations

Women Lawyers of Utah, Inc.
c/o Lisa Michelle Church, Chair
P.O. Box 30825
Salt Lake City, Utah 84130
801-524-2752

Vermont Bar Association
P.O. Box 100
Montpelier, Vermont 05601
802-223-2020

Vermont Bar Association, Women's Section
c/o Julie Brill, Chairperson
109 State Street
Montpelier, Vermont 05609-1001

Virginia State Bar
707 East Main Street, Suite 1500
Richmond, Virginia 23219-2803
804-775-0500

Virginia Women Attorneys Association
c/o Jill Wood, Chairperson
P.O. Box 2465
Richmond, Virginia 23218
804-649-9251

Virginia Bar Association
701 East Franklin Street, Suite 1120
Richmond, Virginia 23219
804-644-0041

Washington State Bar Association
505 Westin Building
2001 Sixth Avenue
Seattle, Washington 98121-2599
206-727-8200

Washington Women Lawyers
P.O. Box 25444
Seattle, Washington 98125-2344
206-622-5585

West Virginia State Bar
2006 Kanawha Boulevard East
Charleston, West Virginia 25311
304-558-2456

State Bar of Wisconsin
402 W. Wilson
Madison, Wisconsin 53703
608-257-3838

Association for Women Lawyers
c/o Carol Comeau, President
1 Plaza East, #709
330 E. Kilborn Avenue
Milwaukee, Wisconsin 53202
414-273-3480

Wyoming State Bar
P.O. Box 109
Cheyenne, Wyoming 82003-0109
307-632-9061

# *Index*

## A

abuse. *See also* domestic violence;
  physical abuse
  in marital torts, 112
  obtaining tape-recorded
    evidence of, 136–38
accountant, avoiding, in
  estimating business, 158
adultery
  costs of, 7
  in determining child custody,
    87
  in establishing fault, 119,
    121–23
  as factor in filing for divorce,
    91–92
  obtaining tape-recorded
    evidence of, 136
  use of credit card receipts in
    proving, 49
  use of private investigator in
    obtaining evidence on, 140
affairs. *See* adultery
age
  of children in determining
    child custody, 82
  as valid reason for
    unemployment, 75

aggravated battery, in marital
  torts, 117
alcohol/drug abuse
  in determining child custody,
    86–87
  in domestic violence, 109–10
  in establishing fault, 119,
    125–29
  use of private investigator in
    obtaining evidence on,
    140–41
alimony, 5–6
  and avoiding appearance of
    cohabitation, 184–87
  avoiding pitfalls in clauses on,
    181–87
  creating reasons for, 74–75
  factors in determining level of, 6
  reasons for termination of, 181
  state laws on, 197–99
  tax treatment of, 79, 173, 178
  termination of, 175
  trend toward short-term, 5
  and unemployability, 69, 70,
    71–72
appeals, 194–95
appraiser, use of, in divorce
  negotiations, 156–57

# Index

interspousal immunity
  abolishment of, 197
  erosion of, 102–3
  state positions on, 102, 198–99
IRAs, setting up, in name, 67–68

## J
job, leaving legitimately, 72–74
judges
  identifying biases of, 23–24
  in making alimony decision,
    5–6
  relationship with lawyer, 21,
    23–24

## L
law clerks, asking for opinion in
  selecting lawyer, 23
lawyer
  articulateness of, 20
  asking for referrals in choosing,
    20–23
  checking out courthouse
    information on, 23
  determining experience level
    of, 21–23
  finding best divorce, 19–32,
    151
  gender of, 22
  identifying biases of judges on,
    23–24
  relationship with divorce
    judges, 21, 23–24
  ties between forensic
    psychologist and, 84
  use of, in hiding assets, 53–54
  waiver of retainer by, 27–28
legal fees
  in challenging
    prenuptial/postnuptial
    contract, 38–39
  level of, 29–30
  for marital tort claims, 104

need for written confirmation
  of, 30–32
payment of by husband, 28–29
timing of payment of, 24–27
waiver of retainer in, 27–28

## M
marital rape, in marital torts, 117
marital residence
  children as factor in awarding
    of, 175–76
  maintenance of, 174–75
marital torts
  abuse in, 112
  aggravated battery in, 117
  civil rights for women in,
    115–18
  definition of, 101
  domestic violence in, 109–10
  effects of
    prenuptial/postnuptial
    agreements on, 108–9
  felony convictions in, 117
  fraudulent inducement to
    marry in, 114–15
  intentional infliction of
    emotional distress in, 106–9
  legal fees for, 104
  marital rape in, 117
  need for corroborating
    evidence in, 104
  negligence in, 113–14
  proving, against husband,
    101–18
  reasons for filing, 103
  revenge as factor in, 6–7,
    107–9
  sexual torts in, 111, 117
  state regulation of, 102–3,
    197–98
  and transmission of sexually
    transmitted disease, 111,
    117

# Divorce War!

use of circumstantial evidence
in, 103–4
marriage length as valid reason for
unemployment, 77
Married Women's Acts, 102
master plan
avoiding admission of, in court,
150–51
avoiding revealing to
psychologist, 165–66
avoiding written evidence of,
149–50
creation of, 7–8, 13–17
keeping secret, 148–49
medical evidence
in proving alcohol or drug
abuse, 127–29
as valid reason for
unemployment, 76
mental abuse and cruelty in
establishing fault, 119, 123–24
military husbands, divorcing, 17
motion for new trial, 193–94

**N**

nagging, as technique to induce
husband to divorce, 96–97
name, setting up IRAs and
retirement accounts in, 67–68
negligence, in marital torts,
113–14
Nineteenth Amendment, 102

**O**

offshore bank accounts, locating
information on, 51
out-of-state property holdings,
locating information on, 51

**P**

payroll stubs, as documentation, 45
personal property
buying on credit cards, 94–96

documentation of, 43–46
investigating and compiling
information on, 41–54
photographing, 42–43
purchasing, with husband's
credit cards, 94–96
state laws on, 198–99
photocopying, business telephone
records, 51
photographic evidence
obtaining, 42–43
in proving alcohol or drug
abuse, 127
in proving physical abuse,
124–25
use of private investigator in
obtaining, 140–41
physical abuse. *See also* abuse
documenting, 109–10
in establishing fault, 119,
124–25
police reports, in providing proof
of physical abuse, 109–10,
124–25
pornography, in determining child
custody, 87
postnuptial contract.
*See* prenuptial/postnuptial
agreements
predivorce acquisition of assets,
60–65
prenuptial/postnuptial
agreements, 33–39
challenging, 35–39
legal fees in challenging, 38–39
and pursuit of marital torts,
108–9
understanding impact of, 39
privacy, and claims of alcohol or
drug abuse, 125
private investigators, 139–45
in documentating cohabitation,
184, 185

222

# Index

money to pay for, 144–45
in obtaining photographic
  evidence, 140–41
qualifications of, 141–43
profit in divorce, 4–6
profit sharing plans,
  investigating, 52
property distribution
  community property versus
    equitable property states,
    197–99
  term cash payments as, 177–78
property settlement agreement
  effect of bankruptcy on,
    173–74
  importance of wording in, 179
  negotiating, 185
psychological evidence
  in proving alcohol or drug
    abuse, 127–29
  in proving emotional distress,
    106–7
  for unemployment, 76–77
psychologist
  avoiding revealing of master
    plan to, 165–66
  criteria for hiring, 164–65
  in documentating alcohol and
    drug abuse, 128
  forensic, 84–85, 162
  payment for, 163
  in proving mental abuse, 124
  in substantiating abuse claims,
    112
  testimony of against husband,
    161–66

## R

rape, marital, 117
real estate, estimating fair market
  value of in divorce
  negotiations, 156–57

rehabilitative maintenance, 5–6.
  *See also* alimony
relatives, lending money to to
  incite divorce, 93–94
retainer, waiver of, 27–28
retirement accounts, setting up in
  own name, 67–68
retirement plans, investigating, 52
revenge as factor in marital torts,
  6–7, 107–9

## S

safe-deposit box, gaining access
  to, 47
savings, protecting predivorce,
  29–30
savings accounts, taking cash
  from, 58–59
secretaries, befriending for gaining
  information, 49–51
sexual requests in determining
  child custody, 87
sexual torts in marital torts, 111,
  117
sibling relationship, in
  determining child custody, 82
split custody, 81
spousal abuse, in determining
  child custody, 83
stockbrokers, befriending for
  gaining information, 49–51

## T

tape-recorded evidence
  admissibility of, 28–29, 138
  avoiding self-incriminating,
    147–48
  in divorce negotiations, 183
  husband's conversations in,
    131–38
  investigating state and federal
    laws about, 132–34